# KENT

Edited by Kelly Oliver

First published in Great Britain in 2003 by
*YOUNG WRITERS*
Remus House,
Coltsfoot Drive,
Peterborough, PE2 9JX
Telephone  (01733) 890066

SB ISBN 1 84460 292 3

# FOREWORD

Young Writers was established in 1991 as a foundation for promoting the reading and writing of poetry amongst children and young adults. Today it continues this quest and proceeds to nurture and guide the writing talents of today's youth.

From this year's competition Young Writers is proud to present a showcase of the best poetic talent from across the UK. Each hand-picked poem has been carefully chosen from over 66,000 'Hullabaloo!' entries to be published in this, our eleventh primary school series.

This year in particular we have been wholeheartedly impressed with the quality of entries received. The thought, effort, imagination and hard work put into each poem impressed us all and once again the task of editing was a difficult but enjoyable experience.

We hope you are as pleased as we are with the final selection and that you and your family will continue to be entertained with *Hullabaloo! Kent* for many years to come.

# CONTENTS

## Hawkhurst CE Primary School

| | |
|---|---|
| Andrew Macdonald (11) | 55 |
| Jamie Briggs (11) | 56 |
| Laura Stone (10) | 56 |
| Megan Graham (10) | 57 |
| Ryan Harris (11) | 57 |
| Sophie Thompson (10) | 58 |
| Steven Beaney (10) | 58 |
| Anna Cragg (11) | 59 |
| Martin Sands (10) | 60 |
| Jessica Buss (10) | 61 |

## Istead Rise Primary School

| | |
|---|---|
| Jack Hanlon (9) | 61 |
| Christopher Thurbin (10) | 62 |
| Alice Toulson (9) | 62 |
| Samantha Brett (11) | 63 |
| Brooke Timms (9) | 63 |
| Stephen Fenniche (10) | 64 |
| Hannah Hatfield (8) | 64 |
| Sam Walker (11) | 65 |
| Matthew Collins (9) | 65 |
| Jake Richards (10) | 66 |
| George Cragg (9) | 66 |
| Alex Dawson (10) | 67 |
| Lucy McCarthy (9) | 67 |
| Thomas Wright (10) | 68 |
| Chloe Gladman (8) | 68 |
| Charlotte Ide (11) | 69 |
| Jodie Brett (8) | 69 |
| Alan McAlpine (9) | 70 |
| Peter Jackaman (8) | 70 |
| Danielle Burton (9) | 71 |
| Lauren Bullen (8) | 71 |
| Adam Tomkins (10) | 72 |
| Billy Butcher (8) | 72 |
| Rebecca Goldsmith (10) | 73 |
| Thomas Merry (8) | 73 |

| | |
|---|---:|
| Joshua Gilleeney  (10) | 74 |
| Courtney Vaughan  (8) | 74 |
| Sydney Moore  (10) | 75 |
| Aaron Wigg  (8) | 75 |
| Katherine Hazel  (10) | 76 |
| Oliver Clark  (9) | 76 |
| Charlotte Thompson  (11) | 77 |
| George Ralph  (8) | 77 |
| Rebecca Dixon  (10) | 78 |
| Emma Bunyan  (10) | 78 |
| Hannah Sewell  (10) | 79 |
| Bethany Charlton  (9) | 79 |
| Stephen Hurdle  (11) | 80 |
| Isla Geis King  (11) | 81 |
| Rebecca Brooks  (10) | 82 |
| Sarah Downes  (11) | 83 |
| James Haigh  (10) | 84 |
| Hannah Merry  (10) | 84 |
| Georgina Hudson  (10) | 85 |
| Franchesca Henry  (10) | 85 |
| Hannah Butler  (10) | 86 |
| Charlotte Stone  (10) | 86 |
| Emily Cragg  (10) | 87 |
| Christopher Treadwell  (10) | 87 |
| Michael Walter  (10) | 88 |
| Hayley Marden  (10) | 88 |
| Liam Smith  (11) | 89 |
| George Rawlings  (9) | 89 |
| Jordan Waterhouse  (11) | 90 |
| Jaime Marsh  (10) | 91 |

### *Langton Green CP School*

| | |
|---|---:|
| Hannah Leeming  (10) | 91 |
| Laura Larkin  (10) | 92 |
| Charlotte Boyd  (10) | 93 |
| Emma Cobbold  (9) | 93 |

### Montbelle Primary School

| | |
|---|---|
| Alice Endersby (11) | 94 |
| Shannon Foley (10) | 95 |
| Hannah O'Connor-Close (11) | 95 |
| Miriam Endersby (11) | 96 |
| Charlotte Appleyard (11) | 96 |
| Sophie Fenlon (10) | 97 |
| Louis Hook (11) | 97 |
| Jamie Brocklehurst (11) | 98 |
| Lucy Wilson (11) | 98 |
| Jade Maloney (10) | 99 |
| Sophie Hutton (10) | 100 |
| Ozay Booth (10) | 101 |
| Danniella Martinez (10) | 102 |

### North Borough School

| | |
|---|---|
| Layla Moore (10) | 102 |
| Sam Berry (10) | 103 |
| Sijan Gurung (10) | 103 |
| Conor Williams-Cooke (9) | 104 |
| Thomas Crickmore (10) | 104 |
| Annabel Farman (9) | 105 |
| Emily Spice (9) | 105 |
| Penny Baker (10) | 105 |
| Luke Sharpe (10) | 106 |
| Ben Wright (10) | 107 |
| Rebecca Batt (9) | 108 |

### Pickhurst Junior School

| | |
|---|---|
| Robert Hogwood (8) | 108 |
| Geneviève Zane (9) | 109 |
| Alex Read (8) | 109 |
| Rory Leader (8) | 110 |
| James Martin (9) | 110 |
| Paul Graham (9) | 111 |
| Amelia Taylor (8) | 111 |
| Joe Darbourne (9) | 112 |
| Marisa Easterling (8) | 112 |

### St Katherine's School, Snodland

| | |
|---|---|
| Jane Bowyer (11) | 135 |
| Craig Curtis (10) | 135 |
| Kirsty Brauninger (10) | 136 |
| Shanee Underdown (8) | 136 |
| Charlotte Huston (8) | 137 |
| Alice White (8) | 137 |
| Charlotte Bungay (8) | 138 |
| Charlotte Phillips (8) | 138 |
| Rhiannon Smith (9) | 139 |
| Natasha Manning (8) | 139 |
| Jorjia Richards (10) | 140 |
| Danielle Edgar (10) | 141 |
| Ryan Williams (8) | 141 |
| Misty Sheldon (11) | 142 |
| Ellis West (8) | 142 |
| Thomas Edwards (11) | 143 |
| Rebecca Merry (9) | 143 |
| Aaron Whatman (10) | 144 |
| Natalie Bush (9) | 144 |
| Aaron Martin (11) | 145 |
| Joshua Allen (9) | 145 |
| Victoria Sopp (10) | 146 |
| Ross Williamson (11) | 146 |
| Kris Deal (10) | 147 |
| Samantha Moore (9) | 147 |
| Joseph Bennett (10) | 148 |
| Christopher Lee (9) | 148 |
| Kirsty Duncan (10) | 149 |
| Kaye Everhurst (11) | 150 |
| Andrew Chambers (9) | 150 |
| Callum Johnstone (11) | 151 |
| Samantha Ripley (11) | 151 |
| Christopher Hover (10) | 152 |
| Beau Ripley (9) | 152 |
| Danielle Balderston (11) | 153 |
| Katy Morgan (9) | 153 |
| Craig Ellis (11) | 154 |
| Emma Allchin (11) | 154 |

| | |
|---|---:|
| Simone Marner (10) | 155 |
| Rebecca Keeley (9) | 155 |
| Rosie-Jane King (8) | 156 |
| Charlotte Sutton (8) | 156 |
| Michael Stevens (9) | 157 |
| Charmaine Tanser (10) | 157 |
| Gary Hanson (10) | 158 |
| Nicole Hill (10) | 158 |
| Lauren Vidler (8) | 158 |
| Ryan Chatfield (10) | 159 |
| Jade Pilkington (10) | 159 |
| Martin Pett (10) | 159 |
| Joe Bottiglieri (11) | 160 |
| Jessica Randall (8) | 160 |
| Ben Chivers (9) | 160 |
| Sophie Ellis (8) | 161 |

**St Michael's CE Junior School, Maidstone**

| | |
|---|---:|
| Jack Kairis (11) | 161 |
| Stephen Smith (10) | 162 |
| Mickayla Ratcliffe (11) | 163 |

**Shernold School**

| | |
|---|---:|
| Charlotte Manzi (11) | 163 |
| Holly Ladd (10) | 164 |
| Lydia Jakob-Grant (11) | 164 |
| Eleanor Oliver (10) | 165 |
| Jade Waymouth (11) | 166 |
| Grace Rudgard (11) | 166 |
| Emily Witney (8) | 167 |
| Isabelle Terry (8) | 167 |
| Pranav Kasetti (8) | 168 |
| Laura Howell (10) | 168 |
| Amy Hartfield (10) | 169 |
| Gina Dimascio (8) | 169 |
| Rebecca Harris (11) | 170 |
| Eleanor Pile (8) | 170 |
| Jenny Cosgrove (10) | 171 |

| | |
|---|---|
| Matthew Burton  (8) | 171 |
| Charlotte Wilmore  (9) | 172 |
| Christabel Webb  (8) | 172 |
| Jessica Rogers  (10) | 173 |
| Nancy Watts  (8) | 173 |
| Tom Cosgrove  (8) | 174 |
| Alice Clarke  (10) | 174 |
| Emma Brand  (8) | 175 |
| Ami-Kay Gordon  (8) | 175 |
| Lourdes Webb  (10) | 176 |
| David Atkins  (10) | 176 |
| Alexandra Browne  (9) | 177 |
| George Edwardes  (10) | 177 |
| Isabelle Loader  (10) | 178 |
| Sophie Howell  (8) | 179 |
| Rhea Tanna  (8) | 179 |
| Harriet Massie  (10) | 180 |
| Lexy Payne  (10) | 180 |
| Jessica Harris  (10) | 181 |
| Michaela Savage  (9) | 181 |
| Rebecca Reardon  (9) | 182 |

### *Sherwood Park Primary School*

| | |
|---|---|
| Rebecca O'Connor  (9) | 182 |
| Karimah Farag  (9) | 183 |
| Samantha Sweeney  (8) | 183 |
| Robert Johnson  (8) | 184 |
| Lucy Ferry  (8) | 184 |
| Taylor Warren  (10) | 185 |
| Alexandra Baxter  (9) | 185 |
| Charlie Elves  (9) | 186 |
| Joey Hosier  (9) | 187 |
| George Poole  (9) | 187 |
| Tom Scott  (9) | 188 |
| Ellie Dobell  (9) | 188 |
| George James  (9) | 189 |
| Sahidur Rahman  (10) | 189 |
| Reni Dare  (7) | 190 |

| | |
|---|---|
| Sian Brown  (10) | 190 |
| Dominic Robson  (9) | 191 |
| Anuska Sivagnanam  (10) | 192 |
| Eleanor Tidnam  (8) | 192 |
| Gala Chan  (10) | 193 |
| Joseph Hamilton  (9) | 193 |
| Katie Glendenning  (10) | 194 |
| Rosie Langridge  (10) | 194 |
| Alexandra Parnwell  (11) | 195 |
| Lucy Walker  (7) | 195 |
| Iain Kemp  (8) | 196 |
| Sophie Gardener  (8) | 196 |
| Tristan Wallace  (10) | 197 |
| Emma Townsend  (7) | 197 |
| Sophie Landick  (8) | 198 |
| Lauren Hopkinson  (8) | 198 |
| Sophie Harrison  (9) | 199 |
| Jake Tucker  (8) | 199 |
| Emily Middleton  (10) | 200 |
| Sam Beach  (11) | 200 |
| Kristy Blackwell  (10) | 201 |
| Lordi Tickell  (8) | 202 |
| Richard Taylor  (10) | 202 |
| Charlotte Campbell  (11) | 203 |
| Ricky Lawrence  (11) | 204 |
| George Cocks  (10) | 204 |
| Colby Ramsey  (10) | 205 |
| Reece Dunlevy  (8) | 205 |
| Catherine Webster  (11) | 206 |
| Billy Batchelor  (8) | 206 |
| Penny Cumbers  (10) | 207 |
| Billy Rixon  (10) | 207 |
| Hannah Nugent  (10) | 208 |
| Jazmine Moss  (9) | 208 |
| Samantha Johnson  (11) | 209 |
| Shreel Patel  (8) | 209 |
| Pinar Coskun  (11) | 210 |
| Jack Quarrington  (10) | 210 |

### The Schools At Somerhill

# The Poems

## LOOKING FROM MY WINDOW

Looking from my window,
I see,
The ripening sky,
The gossiping birds
And the flowers swaying in the breeze.

Looking from my window,
I see
The dancing children,
The proud parents
And a family of foxes watching me.

Looking from my window,
I see,
The glistening dew,
The watery morning sun
And the autumn, yellowing leaves.

*Georgia Corp  (10)*

## THE SCHOOL REPORT

Today in the playground
we are expecting soft snow
falling on the flower bed

Today in the assembly
we are expecting spell of sunshine
lighting up the hall

Today in the corridor
we are expecting lightning
dancing around our heads

Today in the dining hall
we are expecting painful thunder
exploding like volcanoes

After school today
we are expecting
explosions of thunder.

*Jessica Porter  (12)*

## THERE WILL ALWAYS BE TWO OF ME AND YOU

I used to have a dark and lonely room
And forever stay in shadowy gloom.
My mum had said to me, 'Don't go out the alley of black.'
My dad said, 'Down here there is nothing you will lack.'
But then one day I ran out of my boundary of black,
When I reached the light, I stopped and looked back.
I saw an alley as dark as can be
And there attached to my feet was another me.
I was scared because it mirrored whatever I would do,
Wherever I went, wherever I'd go it would come too.
I went back in the alley, it was lost in the black,
I went into the light and the other me was back.
I tried to run, I tried to hide,
But wherever I went, it was there by my side.

Later on, I started school at 4,
I learnt that my number 2, was a shadow
And about shadows I learnt more
And still by my side my shadow will sit,
But now I'm not scared of it, not one bit.

***Kellie Jacques (11)***

## OH NO!

Up to the top of the bus I go,
Whizzing and whizzing about,
Trying to run away from the place
Which I know has a drought.
I'm fed up of no water,
For yet another year and a day,
And so my mum just says,
'Go out and play.'

So up to the top of bus I go,
Trying not to fall over,
As I go to the top of the bus,
The bus which is going to Dover,
Time after time, I try to sit down,
Yet I can't because the chairs keep moving around
And if I try to sit on one,
I find myself on the ground!

I'm almost there, I can see the sea,
But hang on - where's the coast?

*Jonathan Webb (11)*
**Bursted Wood Primary School**

# THE SUPPLY TEACHER

The supply teacher
Walked into the room
We stared at her feature
She was bright blue

She went up to the board
And turned her eyes upon us
And then she called
Up a boy called Ben

Ben didn't get up
He just sat still
He looked like a pup
Who was feeling ill

Then the supply teacher ate Ben
She ate him all in one gulp
Like he was as big as a hen
All of us others ran in fright

Yes, all of us other survived
Except ol' Ben, well, he died
Luckily we weren't caught
This time . . .

*Victoria Tyrie  (10)*
**Bursted Wood Primary School**

## MY WEIRD FAMILY

My weird family
Are really rather strange,
They're never left feeling glum,
I'll describe them to you,
Starting with my mum.

My mum, she is a cleaning freak,
She'd clean every mountain,
Starting at the top peak,
If she had the chance.

My weird family
Are really rather strange,
I'll tell you about the next member,
He's never ever feeling sad,
You'll never guess it's my dad!

My dad, he's rad,
He's really cool,
He makes all the others stop and drool,
He can't move though, his favourite meal is concrete.

My weird family
Are really rather strange
And that's my family,
All of them,
You're probably wondering,
What about me!

***Benjamin Turner (11)***
***Bursted Wood Primary School***

## MICHAELA

Michaela is a kind and caring friend,
Although she drives me round the bend.
She really can be quite sweet and nice,
Although sometimes I wish she didn't eat so many mice.

I have been round Michaela's house
So many, many times,
But then again I wish her other friends
Would not commit so many crimes.

Sometimes Michaela can smell
And I wonder whether she ever washes,
Whenever I give her a wink (just to remind her),
She always goes extremely pink.

Michaela can be very weird,
As last year she told me she was growing a beard.
Michaela is quite short and small,
As when I talk to her, I feel ten foot tall.

*Olivia Gilbert-Smith  (11)*
**Bursted Wood Primary School**

## MY TEACHER

My teacher dances and sings songs
She urges us to all sing along
She jumps and giggles and smiles with glee
In actual fact she frightens me
She likes wearing leather, black to be precise
Sometimes she is rather nice
She shouts at people who've been bad
She makes them feel rather sad
She blows French kisses when she approves
I think she's really smooth
She's not very tall, but she's very loud
She always, always does me proud
She's very cool and I can say
She does things and she does them all her way!

*Emma Price  (11)*
**Bursted Wood Primary School**


## MY GREEDY DOG

I once had a greedy dog,
Who ate and ate like a hog.
He ate tin cans
And mini fans,
My greedy, greedy dog.

I took him for a walk one day
And there in front of us, stood a pile of hay.
He dived right in and ate it all,
He was so round, he looked like a beach ball,
My greedy, greedy dog.

*Georgia-May Barnes  (10)*
**Bursted Wood Primary School**

## First Day Of School

The first day I went to school,
I thought it would be really cool!
Little did I know,
Some bad things were about to show.

I kissed my sweet mother goodbye,
Then jumped for joy really high,
As soon as I got in, they locked the door
And smacked my bottom 'til it was sore.

They shouted at me all the time,
Like I had admitted a vicious crime.
I thought my mum would come soon,
But I was wrong, it wasn't even noon.

They made me eat their horrible lunch,
There were insects in it, *munch, crunch, munch.*
They spilt paint all over my skirt
And my jumper was covered in dirt.

It's nearly home time, I'm so glad,
Those school people make me mad.
Mum said, 'Did you like it dear?'
I said 'No.'
'Oh you'll like it in a day or so.'

'Do you mean I have to go tomorrow?'
'Oh come on, it's not that sorrow.'
'I'm not going back, not any day.'
I know, I'll run away!

*Sarah Avery  (11)*
**Bursted Wood Primary School**

# My School!

At my school it is mean
The classroom is never clean

But when I'm out at play
The sun, it comes to stay

Mrs Dryland is always groaning
Mrs Prynne is always moaning

At my school it is yellow
The classroom is not mellow

And when we do geography
Mr Jones does his biography

Have you seen our light-up screen
From which we read our hymns from?

Mrs Hodder is never moaning
Mrs Hayes you never see groaning

At my school I have school dinners
The children there are winners!

So! Mr Jones is always singing
Miss Joyner is always whinging

And that's my school
But I like it.

*Lauren Campbell (11)*
*Bursted Wood Primary School*

## HOMEWORK

You never bring your homework in,
Your homework's always late,
Don't tell me you dropped it in the bath,
Don't tell me you were on a date.

You never bring your homework in,
Your homework's never done,
Don't tell me you were too tired,
Don't tell me you were reading The Sun.

You never bring your homework in,
Your work is never neat,
Don't tell me that it's writer's cramp,
Don't tell me you wrote it with your feet.

You never bring your homework in,
You never use your pen,
Don't say it's out of ink,
Don't say you wrote it in a fox's den.

You never bring your homework in,
You say you left it by your bin,
What's that next to your desk?
What's happened? You brought your homework in!

*Patrick Beattie  (11)*
**Bursted Wood Primary School**

## FEELINGS

Funny is like gold
It tastes emerald
And tastes like a flower
Funny is a beautiful colour
And it is never dull
It always brings a smile to our face
Funny is never a sad time
And you can have fun with your family

Sad is dull
Like a rainy day
It brings fears to our face
And when you're sad, we are unhappy
And we never smile
Our faces are always down
And we are sad when someone dies
Sad is when no one likes you
Or when you can't do your work
And that's sad.

*Jack Horvath (11)*
**Bursted Wood Primary School**

## PLEASE MR JONES
*(Based On 'Please Mrs Butler' by Allan Ahlberg)*

'Please Mr Jones, this boy Thomas Beales
Keeps calling me names, Sir.
What should I do?'
'Run away to America, run away to sea,
But don't bother me!'

'Please Mr Jones, this boy Arron Such,
Keeps calling me names, Sir.
What should I do?'
'Go to your home, go to Year 4,
But don't bother me!'

'Please Mr Jones, this boy Conar Cooper,
Keeps throwing his rubber at me, Sir.
What should I do?'
'Move next to your friends, run away to the park,
But don't bother me!'

'Please Mr Jones, this boy Rhys Petts,
Keeps on trying to pull my hair, Sir.
What should I do?'
'Run away to the shop and never come back,
But don't bother me!'

'Sir, Sir, Sir.'
'For goodness sake, don't bother me!
Go and sit on the floor,
Oh and don't say Sir!'
'OK Sir, stop saying Sir.'

*Sara Braidwood (11)*
**Bursted Wood Primary School**

## ONE DAY AT SCHOOL

It was just an ordinary school day,
When someone from the school shouted, 'Hey!'
We all ran over in a flash,
To find a dragon giving Mrs Prynne a bash.

Everybody froze with fear,
Some people even had a tear.
Mrs Prynne has bruises everywhere.
A dreadful sight was her hair.

The dragon was ten feet tall
And left a slime mark on the wall.
His eyes were a lovely shade of green,
But his teeth definitely needed a clean.

In came Mrs Dryland with a knife,
Bouncing, jumping, full of life,
She stabbed the knife in his limb
And that was the dreadful end of him.

*Sophie Saunders (11)*
*Bursted Wood Primary School*

## MY TEACHER

My teacher is a man
He's called Mr Jones
And his favourite subject
Is eating ice cream cones

He has brown hair
And wears round glasses
And he cheats in maths tests
No wonder why he passes

He has a different accent
As he comes from Wales
He has a pet cat called Lucy
Who has three tails

He teaches thirty children
And he likes to play a joke
Mrs Dryland thinks he's
A very funny bloke

Everybody likes my teacher
Because he's kind (not!)
And when you get to know him
Better you will find

His desk is a mess
One last thing
About my teacher
Stay away or he will eat ya!
(He's a monster!)

***Kiri Austin-Hall  (11)***
**Bursted Wood Primary School**

## FOOTBALL

No, no, no,
You're doing it all wrong,
You're supposed to test the keeper,
Not play like old Mr Wong.

What a great header,
It just sneaked in,
Next time just
Don't fall in the bin.

What a great save Seaman,
The crowd have gone wild,
When you make a diving save,
The crowd do the Mexican wave.

What great dribbling Pires,
You're a great winger,
You score excellent goals,
Because you're a true winger.

We've won the cup,
We've won the cup,
My team have won the cup,
My team have won the cup.

*Rhys Petts  (11)*
**Bursted Wood Primary School**

# SCHOOL

Children are bright,
They know their rights,
They know the charge,
When they're not at full spark,
They go home in the night.

They get to school
And their teacher's name is Paul,
They know the school,
Around the walls,
They know Paul is cool.

The teachers are small,
The children are tall,
They know the rules,
Some of the children are fools,
The rest are cool.

They are not allowed fizzy drinks,
But still have the whiz,
They are allowed drinks during class,
But we learn fast,
At least we still have the whiz.

*Natasha Gibbs (10)*
**Bursted Wood Primary School**

## SUSEE MALAY

There once was a girl called Susee Malay,
Who flew around the world in a year and a day,
In a hot air balloon she flew in the air
And all she took with her were three sweets and a pear.

When one day she saw an enormous bird,
Its beak was bright green and its feathers absurd,
Its beak burst the ball with a huge *bang*
And down Susee fell to the island of Lang.

There she landed with a bouncy rush,
For she had landed in a purple bush.
Then she heard from this strange little tree,
'Get off you big lump, you are squashing me!'

On the island of Lang, now let me explain,
The sun appears purple and so does the rain,
The trees and the flowers have all learned to talk
And all of the houses have started to walk.

'I need to go home,' cried Susee Malay,
'I said I would be home in a year and a day.'
'No problem,' said the bush out loud,
And with that he bounced her right into a cloud.

Now I can tell you, now I can,
That Susee's tale of the island of Lang,
Around her it is told everywhere,
You could land there, so beware.

***Phoebe Morphew  (11)***
**Bursted Wood Primary School**

## GHOUL SCHOOL

When I go to school
I stare at my teacher
I think she's a ghoul
She puts a shiver down my spine

While I'm working
I sense her lurking
Around me and my best friend, Luke
Instead she opens her mouth and vomits on Duke

I look down on my book
As she breathes on me, dripping blood, my body shook
I knew it, she's a ghoul
And is in our school

Maybe she's a vampire
Who sucks blood of innocent people and causes fire
Where did she come from?
She can't have come from a bomb
Because her name is Mrs Dryland.

*Gurinder Seehra  (11)*
**Bursted Wood Primary School**

## THE BOY

He sat down
And thought he'd drown
Because he had piddled his pants
And in his pants were all the dead ants

This person is a friend of mine
Who once disarmed Calvin Klein
And then shot him in the head
And sprawled him out on his bed

He read a book
To a girl and suddenly said, 'How do I look?'
It's obvious he fancies her
But he only sees her as a blur.

He sips his water
Making sure he only has a quarter
Because he thought he'd piddle his pants
And there would be the dead ants.

*Anthony Sheen  (11)*
**Bursted Wood Primary School**

# MY TEACHER IS A CRAZY TEACHER!

My teacher is a crazy teacher,
Her dancing is her main feature!
I'm sure she has one pretty normal friend,
But she drives us around the bend!
She has a deep dark secret in her mind,
Which everyone in my class wants to find!

My teacher is a crazy teacher,
Everyone knows she's a fabulous creature!
People know that deep in her heart,
All she's ever wanted is a go-kart!
Boogying her body day and night,
Her teaching light shines very bright!

My teacher is a crazy teacher,
Her dancing is her main feature!
Although her teaching goes way too far,
Her favourite subjects are:
Maths, English, science and history,
This teacher's name remains a mystery!

My teacher was a crazy teacher,
Ever yone knew she was a fabulous creature!
She ran away to hide
And news spread that she had died!
My fabulous teacher,
She lived up a wall and no one could reach her!

*Charlie Donovan (10)*
**Bursted Wood Primary School**

## MY DOG, SAM

My dog, Sam
Loves to cook in the frying pan
The food he cooks is great
That's my dog, Sam

He loves to go out on his bike
With his bulldog mate, Mike
The tricks he does are cool
That's my dog, Sam

He's my best friend
Even though sometimes he drives me round the bend
He's really friendly
That's my dog, Sam

He's the best dog anyone could have
I'll never let anyone take him away
He's my dog and friend forever
That's my dog, Sam.

*Lauren Mason (11)*
**Bursted Wood Primary School**

# FEELINGS

Happiness is the colour gold,
It tastes like sugar,
It smells like a scent from a rose,
It looks like a butterfly on a spring day,
It sounds like children laughing,
It feels like a soft animal.

Sadness is the colour grey,
It tastes like sour milk,
It smells like burning rubber,
It looks like a lifeless flower,
It sounds like a steel factory,
It feels like a rough surface.

Shyness is the colour emerald-green,
It tastes like mouldy bread,
It smells like glue,
It looks like a dark, cloudy sky,
It sounds like evil laughing,
It feels like a bumpy surface.

*Conar Cooper  (11)*
**Bursted Wood Primary School**

## OUR SCHOOL IS REALLY WEIRD!

Our school is really weird,
The teachers all have beards,
Mrs Dryland is always prancing
And Mr Jones does ballet dancing!

Our uniforms are stranger
Than Miss Bacon's luncheon manger,
They're blue and purple with rainbow spots,
While the teachers wear tutus, with black and white dots!

Our lunch is very peculiar,
The dinner ladies have arms that are tentacular,
They are huge, green and lumpy
And when they walk past, the floor goes bumpy!

The playground is really strange too,
There is an outside loo,
Our slide points up to the sky
And when you sit on a bench, it flies!

Our head teacher is weirdest of all,
When you're naughty she throws a hard ball,
She has a forked tongue
And yellow hair that is really long!

As you can plainly see,
I need you to rescue me!

*Mercedes Ferguson  (10)*
**Bursted Wood Primary School**

# MY FAMILY

I have a strange family
And also really weird
It's just like I'm having bad luck

My mum does aerobics
But when she bends over
She always splits her trousers

My dad is in the army
He practises his skills
But he keeps on breaking the china

My brother does kick boxing
He does it while he is watching TV
But once he kicked it

My sister does ballet
She does it in her bedroom
She once fell through the floor

My uncle drinks his beer
While he watches TV
And when we get home there's mess on the floor

My auntie does the sewing, she does it all the time
And when we're walking around the house
We always trip over the line

And as for me,
I am practically normal.

***Emma Greatorex  (11)***
**Bursted Wood Primary School**

## JING JANE, THE MONKEY

Jing Jane, the monkey
Look at her scream for more
As she jingles and jangles
On the green tropical floor

There's something going on in the forest
Everyone is looking
The little elephant, the tiger
Leo the lion who is cooking

There is jumping and bouncing
As Jing Jane, the monkey, is bouncing around
As all the animals join and bounce on the ground

Jing Jane, the monkey
Bend her knobbly knees
As she jumps around
On the knobbly tropical trees.

*Georgia Hibbert (10)*
**Bursted Wood Primary School**

## MY FAMILY

My mum does aerobics
But her trousers always split
My dad does lorry driving
But always crashes

My nan goes to church
But always falls asleep and snores
My grandad goes looking for bargains
But he doesn't really want them

My brother does football
But never manages to kick the ball
My sister wears make-up
But always looks like a clown

My auntie goes to the pub
But always falls out the door
My uncle goes boxing
But always comes out with black eyes

My cat stares into the fish bowl
But always gets her head stuck
My dog runs up and down the stairs
But he always falls over

And as for me, well
I am practically normal!

***Cherie Redden  (10)***
**Bursted Wood Primary School**

## MY DINOSAUR

I have a scaly dinosaur,
I like to call him Kit,
Anyone who doesn't like me
Are soon in his stomach pit!

He has an enormous belly,
Because of the children he eats,
When someone is not nice to me, I say,
'Hey, Kit, how about some *treats*?'

He has ferocious claws and fangs,
He does look truly scary,
But inside he is warm and nice,
Also incredibly hairy!

*Luke Verrier  (10)*
*Bursted Wood Primary School*


## THE MAN AND HIS NOSE

I saw a man with a long, long nose
And it was as bright as a red, red rose.
He carried it in a black bag
And even still on it was the price tag.

He never lets it go anywhere
And always looks after it with a lot of care.
Sometimes people often stare,
But they don't really care.

Now I'm getting to the end of the man and his nose,
But keep on reading because this is the poem you chose.
It has turned out to be quite fun
And look, it's even brought out the sun!

*Rachel Gorringe  (10)*
*Bursted Wood Primary School*

# THE KNICKER NICKER

The knicker nicker nicked knickers
Whips them off the line
The knicker nicker nicked my knickers
Hanging out to dry

The knicker nicker nicked Mum's knickers
How? I do not know
The knicker nicker likes big knickers
That make curtains for his show

The knicker nicker nicks my sister's knickers
Who possesses a massive bum
The knicker nicker likes Barbie knickers
He has nicked them from everyone

The knicker nicker nicked Dad's knickers
He is a drag queen you see
The knicker nicker likes men's knickers
Dipped in a cup of tea

Because the knicker nicker nicked our knickers
People chased him in their cars
The knicker nicker doesn't like knickers
He only now likes bras.

*Lana-May Cox  (11)*
**Bursted Wood Primary School**

# MY SWIMMING GALA

On Tuesdays I go for my lessons
Down to my swimming pool
I look on the board, at the list of names
And I see my name typed in bold black ink
I am one of the few
Who has been chosen to swim a gala

The day in question arrives
I have a nervous tingle in my tummy
The time to leave arrives
We set off to the venue

As we arrive, the others are queuing
All nervous and excited
We get changed and walk out to the pool side
I look up at the sea of faces
And see parents wanting winners

My time arrives and I step forward
The whistle blows and I climb onto the block
Silence descends, you can hear a pin drop
My heart is thumping in my chest
I fear that it will burst
The gun goes *bang*
And I hit the water first

I push my hands out and I reach the surface
I take a deep breath
As my head breaks clear
My arms are circling like windmills
And I taste the others' fear

The crowd is going crazy
Shouting, jumping up and down
My body feels as light as air
It cuts through the water like a knife
I can see the end in sight
I reach towards the finish line
With all my might

I feel the side touch my fingers
I pull myself upright
I see the others finishing too
And then it all becomes clear
I am first at the finishing line

*I have won!*

**Georgia Carlton (11)**
**Bursted Wood Primary School**

## FAMILY LIFE

Four flaming members all in
A row: Jamie the greatest,
Ben the buckle and teddy too.
We all play in the green greasy grass.

Ben is the bad one,
He always gets into trouble
And can never get out of it,
So Ben is a big bad boy.

Daddy is the old one,
Mummy's the new one.
I am the weird one,
But all of us put together,
Makes it fun.

**Jamie Povey (10)**
**Bursted Wood Primary School**

## THE SPOOKY BALL PARTY

At midnight they gather up to go to a ball
Which takes place in the haunted hall
They all dance to the boogie song
While the band plays all night long
And the witch grows tall

There is a walking, moaning mummy
Who plays with the talking, chattering dummy
The green gooey gum is jelly
Which goes in your belly
Or tumbles in your tummy

They're shaking their bodies in time to the band
While people are clapping with their hands
As their feet go *tippity-tap*
The baby skeleton sits on its mother's lap
While the ghoulish ghost lands

The vampire drinks real blood
While the sneaky witch causes a dreadful flood
The sly skeleton shows off
And the wicked witch wipes angrily with a cloth
While the witch's books fall into the murky musty mud

The ghoulish ghost flies up in the air
And the werewolf howls and drinks beer
The witch flies on her dirty brown broom
As the children hear a *boom*
All they can see is a witch's hair.

The sun is about to rise
As the spooks all vanish before your eyes
They've had so much fun at the ball tonight
Don't get a fright
They walk out of the spooky ball as the mummy dies.

*Malvin Sawyerr  (11)*
**Bursted Wood Primary School**

## SCHOOL

Sometimes school is such a bore
Especially in RE
We sometimes want to fall asleep
Well in particular me

PE is so much better
Out in the air and the sun
I mean PE in the summer
In winter, it's anything but fun

We also have a whiteboard
They really are great fun
We play educational games on it
ICT is number one

Science is like detective work
With facts we must explore
About germs, guts and gory things
With experiments galore

Our teachers are quite funny
They sometimes act quite daft
Until it's time to get work done
And then they make us graft!

*Daniel Brooker (10)*
**Bursted Wood Primary School**

## SADNESS

Sadness is when the sky goes grey
And all the colours fade away.

Sadness is when the leaves lie
And all the plants begin to die.

Sadness is when the sun turns grey
And the world is black and white all day.

You feel like you're the only one on Earth,
You begin to wonder what it's worth.

Sadness is no birds singing,
Sadness is no laughter ringing.

No beams shining from the pretty sun,
To warm the skin of everyone.

No beautiful sunsets from the skies,
No moon to highlight your sad eyes.

No happy laughter to bring me joy,
No love in the air for this young boy.

*George Davis  (10)*
*Bursted Wood Primary School*

## PLEASE MISS, IT'S GRANDAD'S FAULT!

'Late again Tommy!
You missed the first day of SATs!'

'But, Miss, it's not my fault!'
'Whose is it then?'
'Grandad's, Miss.'
'That makes *twelve* this term,
Nobody has that many!'

'Now, line up for swimming!'
'Can't, Miss.'
'Can't, no such word as *can't* Tommy!'
'No kit, Miss.'
'Where is it?'
'I lost it, Miss.'
'Why can't you get a new one?'
'No money, Miss.'
'Who usually gets your things?'
'Grandad, Miss.'
'Why couldn't he get one?'
'Dead, Miss, all twelve are.'

*Gemma Cannon (10)*
**Bursted Wood Primary School**

## MY TEACHER!

My teacher is the loudest of all,
Though we all think she's really cool.

My teacher makes people really sad,
When they've all been very bad.

My teacher blows us all French kisses
And sometimes even grants our wishes.

My teacher is not very tall,
But doesn't care about being small.

My teacher never eats her lunch,
So during lessons she has a munch.

My teacher is the best of all,
Because she never breaks a rule.

*Emma Varrall  (10)*
**Bursted Wood Primary School**

## OUR TEACHER, MR JONES

Our teacher, Mr Jones
Has a funny accent
Nonetheless we understand it

Our teacher, Mr Jones
Likes to rub his nose
Round and round

Our teacher, Mr Jones
Goes into a daze
And travels far, far away

Our teacher, Mr Jones
Our teacher, Mr Jones
Our teacher, Mr Jones
Is the greatest teacher in the world!

*Jordan Metson (11)*
**Bursted Wood Primary School**


## GEORGE

There once was a spider called George
Who was always very bored
He would crawl about and up the spout
Trying his best to scream and shout
To cheer him up and make him glad
And not to lie so very sad

George decided life would be better
If spiders like him would live forever
Without a care in the world
But for the weather to never be cold.

*Jack Hughes (11)*
**Deal Parochial CE Primary School**

## MY DOG

He is big, black and hairy
With great big white teeth
You would find him scary
But he's a softy underneath
At night he sleeps with me
In my comfy bed
With his tail on the pillow
And his paws on my head!
Once he dug in the garden
He was covered in mud and dirt
Then he went to sleep
On my dad's favourite shirt
He is my very best friend
I think he loves me too
His name is Zeus
The king of dogs
It suits him through and through!

*James Morley (10)*
*Deal Parochial CE Primary School*


## THE MOON

The crescent moon
Crystal silver
Staring with one eye
From the dark of the sky
Into the steely sadness of the night
A silver spider is building his web
Shining in the moonlight.

*Michael Boland (9)*
*Deal Parochial CE Primary School*

# THE LONELY BOY

On the mossy water's edge,
Lays a lonely boy,
With a crumpled newspaper
As his only warmth.

On the mossy water's edge,
Lays a lonely boy,
With the water lapping at his feet
And tears running down his face.

On the mossy water's edge,
Lays a lonely boy,
With a mouldy chocolate bar
And a half-full bottle of juice.

On the mossy water's edge,
Lays a lonely boy,
With a cold and broken heart,
This boy is sure to die.

*Ellis Manning (11)*
**Deal Parochial CE Primary School**


# A SNAKE

It's really, really slippery,
It has scaly skin,
Down the path I walk,
I see its head appear
Out of the green grass,
It comes, getting longer
And suddenly,
There it is a
*Snake.*

*Danielle Jackson (10)*
**Deal Parochial CE Primary School**

## THE BOOK

Just waiting on a shelf to be read,
A dark brown book with dust covering the front,
It has cobwebs hanging off the side,
There are other books next to it,
Blue, tatty and old ones,
Red paperbacks too,
There are mysterious adventures, love lives
And many more books to read to your heart's content.

But why is this book not read?
I didn't hesitate,
I reached over and grabbed it,
On the cover it said, 'Very old comedy jokes',
I turned the first page over,
The jokes were very funny indeed,
I told the librarian that I was going to take this book,
All she said was, 'Alright!'

*Edward Topping (11)*
*Deal Parochial CE Primary School*


## BEES

Bees buzz, bees bash
Bees bang, bees crash
Bees smash, bees mash
Bees boom, bees blow
Bees are wonderful creatures
With stripy colours and wonderful features
I can watch them for hours
As they collect nectar from flowers.

*Christopher Morris (10)*
*Deal Parochial CE Primary School*

## WHERE'S MY GEORGE GONE?

Where's my George gone?
Where's the real George?
I know she's here somewhere,
But where?

She's in the house,
Sitting right next to me,
But in that brain,
She isn't.

Where's my George gone?
Where's the real George?
I know she's here somewhere,
But where?

She's in her bed sleeping,
Until Christmas Eve has gone,
On Christmas Day she awakes,
To find all her presents have gone.

Where's my George gone?
Where's the real George?
I know she's here somewhere,
But where?

I suppose I'll have to wait
Until New Year starts
And hope she'll think what a bad girl
She's been throughout the past.

***Georgina Law  (10)***
**Deal Parochial CE Primary School**

# THERE'S A MONSTER UNDER MY BED!

'Mummy, Daddy, please don't leave,
Don't leave me, please oh please.
I can feel it slithering under me,
It can claw through my mattress with ease.

Mummy, you will leave me,
It'll see you going out of sight,
I'll go to sleep, then suddenly,
It'll get me in the night.'

'Look,' said Mum in angry tone,
'That light's keeping me awake,
We're right next door if you need us,
So get to sleep for goodness sake!'

*Rebecca Larkin  (9)*
*Deal Parochial CE Primary School*


# CAT OF THE NIGHT

The cat of the night shines beneath many twinkling stars,
Her tail for balance as she stalks in the trees,
Her knife-like claws sheathed safely in her delicate paws,
Her prey minding its own business.

The cat of the night shines beneath the glowing moon,
Her glistening starry eyes fixed on her prey,
Her strong hind legs bend back,
Her prey's fate has already been decided.

The cat of the night shines beneath a twinkling deep blue sky,
Her teeth so sharp, concentrating on her meal,
Her pounce so graceful, those few seconds earlier,
Her painful hunger finally satisfied.

*Beth Abercrombie  (11)*
*Deal Parochial CE Primary School*

## THE WAY THE WORLD IS

The world should be a peaceful place
With joy and happiness
Where mouse and cat are best of friend
And deer and lioness

Where no fighting does take place
And everyone obeys
The Ten Commandments God did set
So we can learn each day

But all of this is just a dream
A fantasy world at that
People live such dreadful lives
When one does wrong the other reacts

Oh wouldn't it be harmony
Oh wouldn't it be fun
If everything we look at
Shows the world has just begun!

*Emily Gill  (10)*
*Deal Parochial CE Primary School*


## THE NIGHT LIGHT

The full moon gleams like the sun
It lights up the world below like the reflection on a mirror
It peeps through windows like God watching over us.

*William Dennis  (8)*
*Deal Parochial CE Primary School*

## THE MOON

The moon is white,
The moon is bright,
It's filled with love
And pure delight,
Its fiery blaze
Sets off a craze
And its magnificent light
Shines all through the night!

The moon helps my stepdad
Shoot at night
And when my mum's driving
She can see alright,
But me and my brothers,
The pesky little boys,
Use it for light,
When we end up in fights!

*Elissia Burrows  (10)*
*Deal Parochial CE Primary School*


## JUNGLE ANIMALS

A slithering snake creeping through the leaves
A hairy tarantula sneaking up your leg
A fearsome tiger roaring in the sun
A king of the jungle chasing its prey
And a galloping antelope running away
A herd of elephants stomping along
A tough-skinned rhino with a short temper
With more speed than a sprinting cheetah.

*Natalie Pitcher  (9)*
*Deal Parochial CE Primary School*

## THE HUNTER

A gentle drift of snow falls from the dark grey sky,
A robin perches itself on a bare tree branch,
As a squirrel makes a gentle rustle in a bush.
A gentle patter of rain splashes into a warm, fresh spring,
That laps over the rocks into a frozen pond.
All is quiet till a sudden flock of birds fly overhead,
The animals sensed danger as a hunter entered the forest,
He walked slowly with a gun in his hand,
The snow crunching under his feet,
His gun fired, a poor helpless bird fell out of the sky
And this is how the poem came to die.

*Victoria Wiles  (9)*
*Deal Parochial CE Primary School*


## THE MOON

As I walk down the long, narrow path
I can see the moon shimmering on a *silver* river
Running between two mountains
In the summer you can paddle in the water
Because it is *blue*
And in the winter it's too cold and dark
And it has probably turned to ice
But as the moon shines down on the ice
It looks like a calm field of *green* grass
As I set off home, I can see the moon smiling down at me.

*Molly Green  (9)*
*Deal Parochial CE Primary School*

# THE MOON

The moon is here,
The moon is there,
The moon is simply everywhere,
I look to my left,
I look to my right,
Everywhere I look, the moon is in sight.

When it's dark, I look up and see,
The moon shining over me,
I like to lay in bed at night,
I like the comfort of the moonlight.

Sometimes I stare out of my window
And see the moon high up in the sky,
Surrounded by stars twinkling away,
The brightness of the moonlight leading the way.

It makes me feel safe
Seeing the moon so bright
I snuggle in my bed
And say night-night.

*Lydia Picarelli  (9)*
**Deal Parochial CE Primary School**

# THE MOON

The moon is here
The moon is there
The moon is everywhere
The moon comes out
Like glitter spray
And shines and glitters
Through windows
While children are fast asleep
The moon will come out again
When the sun dies
Then out comes the moon
Like a silver ball.

*Bethany Robson  (8)*
*Deal Parochial CE Primary School*


# FRIENDSHIP

Friendship is about caring for your friend
Looking after them if they're ill or sad
And always being by their side

If you are a girl and you're friends with a boy
It doesn't matter
As long as you're nice to each other

You don't have to look the same
Or like the same things
You just have to like each other
Because if you don't like each other
You will be in misery.

*Abigail Pearn  (9)*
*Farnborough Primary School*

## HANNAH!

She is trustworthy,
I can tell her my secrets.
She is kind to me
And I am to her, (I think).
That's my friend, Hannah,
She's very respectful,
Cares for all my things.
She's loyal to me,
She will stick up for me,
That's my friend, Hannah.
She has a helping hand,
If I fall over, she'll use that hand,
She shares with me
And gives me anything.
That's my friend, Hannah,
She is honest
And tells me if it's right.
If I am feeling down,
I know she'll cheer me up,
That's my friend, Hannah.
She'll give me support,
When the going gets tough,
This girl is important to me,
I love her as a friend,
That's my friend, Hannah.
She is playful,
We'll play all day,
She is very pretty,
She will win all the boys,
She's the best ever,
That's my friend, Hannah.

*Rachael Adams (9)*
*Farnborough Primary School*

## FRIENDSHIP IS GREAT!

F riendship is the greatest
R especting things is good
I like friends that are honest
E specially my friends that would
N eed to chat
D efinitely my friends will be there
S ometimes I can be a bad sight
H ey, my friends don't care!
I like to have a good laugh
P laying with my friends as well

I like to gossip on the phone
S ometimes there are secrets to tell

G race and Sam are going out
R ebecca and David kissed!
E ven though we do break up
A t times we can be missed!
T ogether forever, our friendship will last!

*Rebecca Thwaites  (9)*
*Farnborough Primary School*


## FRIENDSHIP

F riendship is very important.
R espect your friends so that they respect you.
I 'm very happy to have this friend.
E very friend may not be *the* friend.
N ice friends are the best, like this friend.
D o you know I have a best friend called Andrew Whiting?
S o I'll see you later, bye.

*Daniel Hughes  (10)*
*Farnborough Primary School*

## FRIENDSHIP

Friends are important,
They help you if you are in trouble
And badly need help.
I say if my friend doesn't look good in some clothes
And my friend says if I look good and if I don't.
She makes me feel better,
She cares for me as well.
Sometimes we break up,
But we don't tell our secrets.
My friend always tells the truth,
If someone has upset me,
She makes me feel better,
If she's upset, I make her feel better.
My friend is Charlotte Couchman.

*Lindsay Ferdinando  (9)*
*Farnborough Primary School*


## FRIENDSHIP

Trust is
Very important,
You should
Always trust
Your friends,
If you can't trust them,
You can't have a friend,
You can
Tell them anything,
Trust them and
They will trust
You back.

*James Snow  (9)*
*Farnborough Primary School*

## FRIENDSHIP

The feelings of your friends bring you joy,
The feelings of your friends bring you hope,
The feelings of your friends bring you joy and hope,
They must be really good friends.

Friends have feelings for you and themselves,
Friends have respect for you when you feel bad,
Friends have support for you whenever you feel sad.

Friends say compliments when you feel bad,
Friends make you feel happy when you feel sad.

Friends always are with you when you feel alone,
Friends always are with you when you don't feel at home.

Friends play with you when you are alone,
Friends give you courage when you feel scared.

Friends tell you good things,
Friends tell you things that are bad,
Friends tell you when they are happy
And when they are sad.

Friends play with you when you feel alone,
Friends talk to you when you are on the phone,
Friends try to be good to you
And friends cheer you up.

I always try to be a good friend,
Even when they drive you round the bend.

I try to do all of them,
I hope I am a really good friend.

*Sarah Richards (9)*
*Farnborough Primary School*

## FRIENDS

There're a lot of different friends that you can have,
Boyfriends and girlfriends, your mum and your dad.

The girl from your dance class who's happy and bright,
The boy from that football team you're playing Friday night.

There're friends who stick by you, through happy and sad,
Friends who never complain even when you're driving them mad.

Friends who ring you up with the gossip from school,
Friends who don't make fun of you, whether you're big
                                        or skinny and small.

Annoying boys who sit next to you, they're not that bad I suppose,
They're just trying to be friends, so we've got to put up with
                                        them when they pick their nose.

If you ever have an argument, don't be afraid to say sorry,
If your friendship is strong enough, no fights can destroy it, so
                                        you don't need to worry.

What I'm trying to say is this, never take your friends for granted,
Just make sure your relationship lasts, 'cause a friendship flower
                                        has been planted.

***Lauren Plummer  (10)***
***Farnborough Primary School***

# WHAT FRIENDS MEAN TO ME!

She means love and kindness
She can share
She'll be helpful, when I am sad
She'll always be there; there for me
She'll always be kind; kind to me
She is friendly
She is Maria

He is loyal
He can help
He is friendly always to me
He'll be kind; kind to me
He will let me, let me join in, join in all his games
As well, I will let him join in my games
He is Chris

She is my teacher and I like her
She can be kind and a bit *loud!*
She is my teacher
She stands out
She is Mrs Harrison
And I like her

She is a teacher
She helps Daniel
She is kind and likes chocolate
I am cheering her on to lose weight
She is Mrs Nunn.

**Stephanie Bacon  (9)**
**Farnborough Primary School**

## FRIENDSHIP

A   is for Abi, my best friend,
B   is for being a really good person,
C   is for crazy, she is round the bend,
D   is for daring, no, she's not really this,
E   is for enjoy, she's really very witty,
F   is for fun, a humorous kind of girl,
G   is for green thumb, she likes gardening a lot,
H   is for honest, she's the person anyone would want,
I    is for Iceland, we both want to go there,
J    is for jelly, she likes it loads,
K   is for kind, she is very, very, very kind,
L    is for lollies, she has loads in her lunch,
M   is for money, she gets pocket money,
N   is for naughty, we're both this,
O   is for older, only by a few months,
P   is for prize, she should have one,
Q   is for Queen, we both want to be her,
R   is for rabbiting down the phone,
S    is for sharing, she can really do this,
T   is for trust, I can tell her anything,
U   is for understanding problems,
V   is for very pretty, which she is,
W   is for wonderful to have around,
X   is for an extraordinary friend,
Y   is for *errr* . . . I think I'll miss this one out,
Z   is not for . . . the end!

*Charlotte Tytler (9)*
*Farnborough Primary School*

## FRIENDSHIP

I show my friends love, I never push or shove,
They know I would run a mile, just to see them smile.
She's like a flower dancing in a shower of rain,
That's my friend, Rachel.
She sometimes is a pain, but we always become friends again.
She's like a toy that brings you joy.
That's my friend, Rachel.
If you were a bird coming to land, there she would be,
Ready to give you a helping hand,
That's my friend, Rachel,
We always share and play fair.

*Hannah Steggle (9)*
*Farnborough Primary School*


## LIFE

Life is like a day,
Starting and finishing.
It begins in the morning,
When the sun awakes from a deep sleep,
A new life starts.
Your childhood is midday,
You are growing up and having fun.
Middle age is the warm mid-afternoon sun.
Your older years are the cool early evenings,
Old age creeps up quickly.
A new day ends and so does another life,
As a new one begins.

*Andrew Macdonald (11)*
*Hawkhurst CE Primary School*

## WHAT AM I?

Am I the sun that blazes
   Or am I the moon that shines with the stars?
Am I the wind that whistles through the air
   Or am I the thunder that crashes and bangs?
Am I the sea that laps the shore
   Or am I the river that flows past
Am I the earth that grows the flowers
   Or am I the flower of beauty and passion?
Am I the tree of power and glory
   Or am I the bush of love and friendship?
Am I the grass that sways to and fro
   Or am I the hay that feeds the animals?
Am I the animals, great and small
   Or am I the ant small, but wise?
Am I the house that is warm and cosy
   Or am I the furniture, all nice and clean?
Am I the bed, cosy and soft
   Or am I the child asleep in the bed?
Shall I tell you who I am?

*I am your dream.*

**Jamie Briggs (11)**
**Hawkhurst CE Primary School**


## SOOTY

Sooty is a very funny cat,
At night she sleeps on the fluffy mat,
She used to catch mice,
That's not very nice,
When she is good, we give her a pat.

**Laura Stone (10)**
**Hawkhurst CE Primary School**

## Sailing In Dolphin Waters

I stood on deck, the sun was shining
I missed the land, my heart was pining

It was just then something caught my eye
Was it a bird up in the sky?

I looked up, the sky was clear
Beneath our ship the dolphins were here

Swiftly, silently, their bodies shimmered
Beneath the waves the ocean glimmered

Leaping up out of the sea
Showing off to you and me

My spirit lifted, I had to smile
Good luck they bring with such style

We sailed on into the sun
Until they left having had their fun

Alone I stood, sad no more
For now I knew we'd reach the shore.

*Megan Graham (10)*
*Hawkhurst CE Primary School*


## The World

The world is such a wonderful place,
Have you seen the moon's sparkly face?
There's so many animals in the world,
Some are fat, some are small,
Some are tiny, some are tall.
There are giant elephants and tiny snakes,
There are crocodiles and snowflakes.

*Ryan Harris (11)*
*Hawkhurst CE Primary School*

## SPRING IS COMING

Spring is coming
With leaves indeed,
The farmers should be sowing
All of their seeds.
Buds are bursting,
Lambs are leaping,
All through time,
The spring is keeping,
Spring is coming,
End of the winter,
The wonderful spring,
Time to enter.
Daisies are growing
In the ground everywhere,
They can be picked,
To show and to share.

*Sophie Thompson  (10)*
*Hawkhurst CE Primary School*


## MYSTERY

One night when it was quite late
I thought I heard the garden gate
Whilst waiting for a knock at the door
I swallowed my apple core
I coughed and spluttered and went quite red
And woke up in my bed
What a dream it must have been
For Father Christmas I hadn't seen.

*Steven Beaney  (10)*
*Hawkhurst CE Primary School*

# FLOWER POWER

I am the poppy,
Small, round and friendly,
Emblem of peace,
Gathering in fields tenderly.

I am the foxglove,
Sly, sharp and sleek,
Velvet cups of silky pollen,
Tempting you to sleep.

I am the rose,
Fluffy, pink and smiley,
What a beautiful head I produce,
I catch you out slyly.

I am the lily,
Fiery, red and mad,
A sheet of flame over my head
And being a lily, I'm glad.

I am the sunflower, king of all the flowers,
Golden beams of sunlight,
Giving pleasure for hours.

But I am just a forget-me-not,
Forgotten, small and blue,
I still have the almighty beauty,
That keeps all flowers true.

*Anna Cragg  (11)*
*Hawkhurst CE Primary School*

## FEELINGS

A white football,
A lost shuttle.
A strawberry,
A pool of blood.

A massive crash,
Through the roof,
It was a cannon ball,
I stood petrified.

A hubcap from
A car,
The helmet of
A stuntman.

A smashed dish,
With ducks on it,
It must be thrown,
(Should be anyway),
It's replaceable,
To go on the fireplace,
Lovely.

*Martin Sands (10)*
*Hawkhurst CE Primary School*

## ANIMALS

Animals come in many shapes and sizes,
Sharp teeth and beaks,
Roars and squeaks
And fur and scales as their disguises.

Some have paws
And some have claws,
Some walk on two feet
And some on more feet.

We keep some as pets
And some on the farm.
We take them to the vet's,
To keep them from harm.

*Jessica Buss  (10)*
**Hawkhurst CE Primary School**


## THE WEATHER

The weather is big, the weather is strong,
Sometimes reports are mostly wrong.
Today's forecast, sunny and bright,
But it will become colder at the start of night.
Around the world, people worry
There could be a storm and it could come in a hurry.

*Jack Hanlon  (9)*
**Istead Rise Primary School**

## WEATHER

Children playing in the snow
Having laughs and lots of fun
Building snowmen and
Snowball fights
Sliding down the mountain slope

Now the snow has
Turned to ice
Children skate
On the ice
Animals slipping and
Falling over

Now the snow and
Ice has thawed
Rain is falling and
Children are getting wet
Animals hide from pouring rain

Now the thunder has begun
Babies cry for their mums
Dogs bark
Cats hide
Wild animals run for shelter.

*Christopher Thurbin  (10)*
*Istead Rise Primary School*


## SUNNY SKY

The sun woke from a long nap
The sun woke up from a cloud
The sun is bright
So everyone is happy again.

*Alice Toulson  (9)*
*Istead Rise Primary School*

## TWIST AND A TWIZZLE

Leaves rustling, winds blowing,
Storms are heading this way,
Even though it's May,
No sun any day, just rain,
People think a twister is going to come
And one of those people is my mum!

Thunder, lightning, here it comes,
Twist and a twizzle,
Sizzle round, it's going like a spinning top,
Trees flying everywhere,
Children screaming and crying,
Other people saying 'Wahoo!'
The weather, getting colder every minute,
Lakes are freezing up,
A soft breeze hits our faces,
The twister has gone,
Everyone happy again as it starts to rain!

*Samantha Brett (11)*
*Istead Rise Primary School*


## CLOUD WITH SUN

White or grey,
The clouds might be.
Hopefully they will be -
Light with glee!

Sunny, sun, sun, come out to play,
Shine over the Earth for the rest of the day.
When night falls,
The day repeats on and on and on.

*Brooke Timms (9)*
*Istead Rise Primary School*

# NORTH, SOUTH, EAST AND WEST

Today in the south,
There will be sun and clouds.
So splash on the cream
And get bikinis out!

Across to the west,
Keep on your vest
Because they'll be rain and wind,
Blowing right through your skin!

Up in the north,
There will be gale force winds,
So glue your hats on,
Or spend the weekend in!

Across to the east,
There'll be a beast of a storm,
So get your umbrellas out
And raincoats too.

This is the forecast,
For the next few days.
So goodbye from me,
I'll see you again.

*Stephen Fenniche (10)*
*Istead Rise Primary School*


## UNTITLED

The sun appears so bright and yellow
Masked by a cloud, fluffy and grey
Sun, so hot like an oven
It should stay out all day.

*Hannah Hatfield (8)*
*Istead Rise Primary School*

# RAIN

The grass is wet,
The clouds are grey,
There's nothing to do
On a rainy day.
The rain comes down,
The puddles are dirty,
The sun has gone,
The air is murky,
I look out of the window
And all I see is
Just tiny drops of rain,
Spitting at the ground.
If it doesn't stop soon,
It will start to flood,
I'm really, really worried,
Please stop soon.
The river has overflowed,
The sandbags are out,
That's rain for you,
It just won't stop.

*Sam Walker (11)*
**Istead Rise Primary School**


# LIGHTNING BLASTS

Lightning, lightning, burning bright
Blasting through the winter's night
Better watch out, you're in for a fright
Blasting from a tall height
Then it goes out of sight.

*Matthew Collins (9)*
**Istead Rise Primary School**

## THE TORNADO

Twist and twizzle, round and round,
*Bang, smash, wallop*, destroyed a town,
Leaving destruction wherever I go,
Twist and twizzle, here I go,
You can't catch me, I'm on the run.

Twizzle, twizzle, twizzle, round and round,
Run, run, run, I'm coming,
With a thunderstorm cloud,
Hungry for houses, hungry for people,
Yum, yum, yum, I'm very lethal.

Faster than a plane, *zoom, zoom, zoom*,
Through villages and cities,
Watch out people, I'm coming for victims.

*Jake Richards (10)*
*Istead Rise Primary School*


## STORMY STORM

Breakfast -
Here is the rain time
Lunchtime -
Here is the thunder time
Night-time -
I see the lightning time
The next day the sun came out
And becomes our friend again.

*George Cragg (9)*
*Istead Rise Primary School*

## A NONSENSE POEM

In Aberdeen it's going to snow,
. . . so dig out those trunks.
In Bognor it's going to be sunny,
. . . so hunt for your toboggan.
In London it's going to be windy,
. . . so just right for sweeping up the leaves.
In Cornwall there are going to be 8ft high waves,
. . . so why not go for a swim.
In St Andrews it's going to be great for golf,
. . . as lightning is predicted.

In Bridgetown-Barbados it's going to be foggy,
. . . so great for sightseeing.
In Hawaii they've got hailstones the size of footballs,
. . . so good for topping up your tan.
In Austria all the snow has melted,
. . . so Austria is the place for skiing.
In Egypt sandstorms are blowing up,
. . . so great for a camel ride in the desert.
In Siberia it's -33°C and falling,
. . . so don't forget your suntan lotion.

*Alex Dawson  (10)*
*Istead Rise Primary School*


## WEATHER

Brightly the sun shines
Over the Earth
To make people jolly
And enjoy their work.

*Lucy McCarthy  (9)*
*Istead Rise Primary School*

## WEATHER POEM

The lightning crashes
The thunder comes bolting down

Rain and the hail
Wakes the dead
When the cars roar down the roads

The rain that
Pitter-patters on the ground
It drives people barmy
It floods and freezes
The ponds

The hail that
Crashes and smashes
On the pavement
It's hard ice
And it comes down heavily

The thunder and lightning
Gives you a scare

People hate this
Kind of weather.

***Thomas Wright (10)***
**Istead Rise Primary School**


## RAIN

Sun, sun, come out to play
Tell the clouds to go away
Why don't you all come and play?

***Chloe Gladman (8)***
**Istead Rise Primary School**

## THE SNOW HORSE

The light fluffy snow falling from the air,
Falling on the ground and then resting there,
Then as people walk across the snow,
It makes a crunching sound.

I'm standing there alone, leaning on a fence,
Staring at a dapple grey,
It was neighing, its head was held high,
Paused in mid-flight as if it knew
I had seen it and was glad.

The snow was starting to fall and fall,
So I went back home,
The image of that beautiful horse
Silhouetted against the pure white snow,
Knowing I would never forget that beautiful horse,
The snow horse,
I love snow.

*Charlotte Ide  (11)*
*Istead Rise Primary School*


## CLOUDY SUN

Clouds, clouds go away
Tell the sun to come and play
Sun, sun come here
Come today to play all day
It's getting dark
Tell the moon
To come out soon.

*Jodie Brett  (8)*
*Istead Rise Primary School*

## WEATHER

Waking from a long nap
A bright star lit
It shone high above
A grey mist
Tears of water fall from above
Human seeks shelter
Heating with love
We've been safe all day
All the children start to play.

*Alan McAlpine  (9)*
**Istead Rise Primary School**


## CLOUDY

In the floating sky
Where the fluffy white cloud lays
Very still and dry
And as I gaze
The sky is grey
And at night
The cloud goes away
When I go to bed
It gives me a fright
When the stars are there instead.

*Peter Jackaman  (8)*
**Istead Rise Primary School**

## WEATHER

A cloud-covered star shone brightly
Slightly the cloud began to make way
For the star so bright came through so tightly
The people of Earth shouted 'Hooray'
But the cloud wasn't finished
It roamed in front of the star
The star thought it was the brightest
But then a great wind blew from afar
It blew the cloud away, soon it was gone
The star was safe
By the way, the star is the sun!

*Danielle Burton  (9)*
*Istead Rise Primary School*


## UNTITLED

Thunder, thunder, burning bright
Rushing through the winter's night
Let's hope it doesn't strike

Rain, rain, dropping light
Lightning, lightning, burning bright
Through the breezy night.

*Lauren Bullen  (8)*
*Istead Rise Primary School*

## BAD WEATHER

If the weather is bad
People are sad
Sitting at home
Bound to a stone
When the weather is bad

People are weary
And looking all dreary
Wish there was sun
Having no fun
When the weather is bad

Rain, snow and hail too
All put on this earth to torment you
The wind nearly blows
You out of your clothes
When the weather is bad

People are keen to
Dream, dream, dream
When they're looking out of the window
Because they've never been so sad
When the weather is bad.

*Adam Tomkins (10)*
*Istead Rise Primary School*


## STORM

Storm, storm, go away,
You may be dark and rainy,
You may have lightning
And you may be big,
But I'm not afraid of you.

*Billy Butcher (8)*
*Istead Rise Primary School*

## NONSENSE POEM

It's tot today
No need for dumpers
Time for spimsuits
And barbecues
You may beed sun cream
The weather fourcast says its' going to be told tommoray
Oh no is dot rain
Not again!
Better gett tinside
I tate rain
Pain, pain, go away
Come pack anover day
The sun's back, yeah
It's tot today
No need for dumpers
Time for spimsuits.

*Rebecca Goldsmith (10)*
*Istead Rise Primary School*


## SUNNY SKY

The sun went in
And the moon came out
Darkness again until
Another day in the morning.

*Thomas Merry (8)*
*Istead Rise Primary School*

## GUESS WHAT IT IS?

It twists and twists and twists,
Blows you away,
Blows anything away!

It swirls and swirls and swirls,
Takes anything with it as it swirls,
Zooming past like a speeding bullet,
With everything I know of;
Cows, sheep, houses, fences, gates
And many other things.

It whirls and whirls and whirls,
Like a very, very fast spinning top,
That travels around lots of cities around the world.

It's spinning and spinning and spinning,
Like a dizzy dinosaur in the prehistoric times.

*Joshua Gilleeney (10)*
*Istead Rise Primary School*


## WEATHER

When it's cloudy
When it's wet
I couldn't find my favourite dress
I'm always in a mess
The sun came out
I gave a shout
And then I was very glad
Because I was very mad.

*Courtney Vaughan (8)*
*Istead Rise Primary School*

## RAIN POEM

Rain dripping down
*Drip drop*
On people's houses
*Drip drop*
People with umbrellas
*Drip drop*
Rain coming from black clouds
*Drip drop*
Rain rushing down gutters
*Drip drop*
And down drains
*Drip drop*
Falls into rivers
*Drip drop*
Also into streams
*Drip drop*
Sun sucks up rain
*Drip drop*
Goes back into clouds
*Drip drop*
And it all starts again
*Drip drop.*

**Sydney Moore  (10)**
**Istead Rise Primary School**


## THUNDER BLAST

Thunder, thunder, burning bright,
In the day, near the night,
Bet it will give you a fright
And disappear out of sight.

**Aaron Wigg  (8)**
**Istead Rise Primary School**

## WHAT AM I?

*Pitter patter* through the kitchen
Slip out the door
To the outside
Where I make mischief

Jump over the fence
Where the mice play
One, two, three, *pounce!*
My lunch is made

My human doesn't know where I've been
As I slip back inside
They greet me like I've never gone
I curl up by the fire

Now it's dinnertime
I'll tell you what I am
I'm a fat old moggy cat
Who has far too much to eat!

*Katherine Hazel  (10)*
**Istead Rise Primary School**


## STORM

Angry, booming,
Thunder blended with
The flashes of lightning
Rainy splashes,
Noisy bullet,
To the ground.

*Oliver Clark  (9)*
**Istead Rise Primary School**

## RAIN

The rain is falling down
*Drip, drop, drip*
Rain everywhere to be seen
Flooding the ground
The place is out of bounds
All different sounds all around
The hounds in their home safe and sound
Trees blowing in the breezy wind
Leaves flowing in the rain
Going down the drain
The rain is starting to chuck down
Oh no, not again!

The sky is dark and dull
Clouds moving to and fro
The moon is not to be seen
All you can see is the rain falling down on me
Soaked right through
Oh, what am I going to do?
Kicking the rain with my feet
When the rain is falling down on me.

***Charlotte Thompson  (11)***
**Istead Rise Primary School**


## THE SUN AND CLOUDS

After a long and dark night,
Something appeared that was bright,
Then a dark blob came
And now it is pouring with rain,
I wonder if it will be wet all day?

***George Ralph  (8)***
**Istead Rise Primary School**

## THE WOLF-LIKE WIND

The wolf-like wind howls,
While desperate for warmth are the cows,
The swans and geese have all flown south,
The rivers and ponds look like a huge dark mouth.

Horses huddle close together in the cold,
The fields have not enough grass to hold,
The sheepdog's limbs are stiff and frozen,
He can't believe that out of all his brothers, to chase sheep
                                    he was chosen!

A strike of lightning hits the sky,
As a cart pony starts to shy,
A grand old oak gets hits by lightning,
With flames licking the branches, it's very frightening!

*Rebecca Dixon  (10)*
*Istead Rise Primary School*


## MY ANIMALS

My dog, Lucky has long black ears
And a little black nose,
My rabbit, Flopsy has a small fluffy tail
And plays football.
My guinea pig, Midget is not that big
And she squeaks a lot,
That's my animals.

*Emma Bunyan  (10)*
*Istead Rise Primary School*

## MY DOGS ARE NUTTY

My dogs are nutty,
They chase their tails,
Try and eat snowballs,
Not mentioning snails.

My dogs are nutty,
They play hide-and-seek
Can't play fetch
And bark in my ear - *eeeeek!*

My dogs are nutty
They bark at the doorbell
Love to go on walks
Do loads more silly things, but I won't tell!

**Hannah Sewell  (10)**
**Istead Rise Primary School**


## THE SOMETHING

From a cloud appearing,
Something shining,
Something bright,
Something that never comes out at night,
The cloud is dull,
Misty grey,
But now joyful,
Ready to play.

**Bethany Charlton  (9)**
**Istead Rise Primary School**

# GOAL

Sam to Adam
Adam to Liam
Liam to Owen
Owen to Jack
It's a gaol, 1-0

Jake to Ashley
Ashley to Kenny
Kenny to Martin
Martin to Josh
It's a goal, 1-1

Halftime
The subs are
Owen for Stephen
And
Liam for Ashley

Sam to Adam
Adam to Liam
Liam to Stephen
Stephen to Jack
It's a goal, 2-1

Fulltime
The score was 2-1
To Stephen's team
Well done, Stephen
Thank you.

*Stephen Hurdle  (11)*
*Istead Rise Primary School*

## THOSE WERE THE DAYS

Those were the days when we all had friends,
Those were the days when fun knew no ends.
Those were the days when there was laughter,
Those were the days when we leapt and looked after.
Those were the days when we strolled through the grass,
Those were the days when troubles came last.
Those were the days when happiness ruled,
Those were the days when around we fooled.
Those were the days when silver was gold,
Those were the days when young turned to the old.
Those were the days when the torch we held,
Those were the days when tolled did the bells.
Those were the days when we'd no need to listen,
Those were the days when the rivers did glisten.
Those were the days when all could be trusted,
Those were the days when bread was brown crusted.
Those were the days when we drank clear water,
Those were the days when down the roads we did saunter.
Those were the days when the birds sang out loud,
Those were the days when the fox chased the hound.
Those were the days when the cock crowed at dawn,
Those were the days when the farmer grew the corn.
Those were the days when all were rich,
Those were the days when all tents we could pitch.
Those were the days when all clothes were soft cotton,
Those were the days when no food became rotten.
Those were the days when all the leaves rustled,
Those were the days when all people bustled.
Those were the days when we went our own ways,
Those were the days, well, those were the days!

*Isla Geis King (11)*
**Istead Rise Primary School**

## SUCH A CHANGE

Quietly the snow gently appears
It falls to Earth like white tears
It covers the land making no sound
And lays silently all around
Virgin white, pure and bright
The snow laid making life so very quiet.

Silently a blanket comes to Earth
A blanket made of swirling fog
It nestles down upon us
Swirling, twirling, grey and white
The fog settles down for the night
Alone and still you cannot see
Not even the distant garden trees
The fog laid making life so very quiet
But sometimes you can see a pinprick of light.

Violently, with force, it hits the ground
The rain beats everything all around
The wind picks up, the rain increases
It seems it never ceases
Ferociously the trees are swaying
In all directions they are moving
The rain fell making life so very loud.

Brightly the rays shine upon the ground
It warms the earth and all around
It gives you hours of sunlight too
Making all the flowers bloom
It seems not to last for many days
So we spread ourselves out to catch the rays
We worship the sun for days and days
But like anything the seasons change.

***Rebecca Brooks (10)***
***Istead Rise Primary School***

## BLOW AWAY THE MOONLIGHT

Flying in all directions,
She gallops on happily,
She's free and proud,
While no one is around.

Floating in and out,
She prowls along in a glorious mood,
No one knows she is there,
While she creeps on unheard.

Someone is there,
While she's trotting over to the bush,
She never saw a thing,
Apart form a tiny butterfly.

Creatures stop and stare,
As she glides along the ground,
Not hearing a thing,
Apart from a tiny little ladybird.

She gallops on freely,
Not seeing a thing,
But a group of animals in the distance,
No one can see her, not even a glimpse.

*Sarah Downes (11)*
*Istead Rise Primary School*

# D-DAY

See the boats in the distance
A shower of bullets flying over you
Hit the shore with a *crash*
You plunge into the sea and take cover

All you hear are guns firing
You and your friends fire mortars
To get through the wall
The wall breaks
Suddenly a spray of bullets goes through

As you run through the town
Killing Germans on the way
You creep through alleyways
Climbing the tower with slippery steps
All the way to the top.

*James Haigh  (10)*
**Istead Rise Primary School**


# MY DANCING FEET

My hands start clapping,
My feet start tapping,
My body starts to groove.

It's non-stop,
I dance till I drop.

When I hear the funky beat,
I show off with my moves.

It's non-stop,
I dance till I stop.

*Hannah Merry  (10)*
**Istead Rise Primary School**

## FREEDOM OF A HORSE

I wish I had the freedom of a wild horse,
The wish to run wild and free,
To fight off danger and celebrate my victory in glee,
To toss my mane to and fro,
To neigh and whinny as I go.

The wish to gallop for as long as I like,
To tell the hunters to take a hike.
The wish to run through the lush summer grass,
To beat everyone who challenges me because I'm too fast!

*Georgina Hudson (10)*
*Istead Rise Primary School*


## MY CAT

My cat is very funny,
He even has his own money,
My cat is very cool,
He even sits in a pool,
My cat is very nice,
Only thing . . . he hates mice!
My cat gets in a mood,
But what calms him is food!
My cat would like
To ride a bike,
My cat only likes . . .
*Me!*

*Franchesca Henry (10)*
*Istead Rise Primary School*

## SNAILS

They are small and slide along the ground
And leave silver slimy trails,
They eat leaves and munch all day,
They could only be the snails!

They have shells that swirl around
And leave silver slimy trails,
They eat people's plants and flowers,
They could only be the snails!

They are small and slide along the ground
And leave silver slimy trails,
They eat people's plants and flowers,
They could only be the snails!

*Hannah Butler  (10)*
*Istead Rise Primary School*


## IN THE CAR

In the car I can
See lots of things
Out of the window
Things here
Things there
Things everywhere
Some are scary
Some are cute
And some are very ugly.

*Charlotte Stone  (10)*
*Istead Rise Primary School*

## SHADOWS

The shadows in the corner,
Give me quite a scare,
They're in the big, big wardrobe
And underneath the stair!

I have never dared look,
Underneath my bed,
While lying in the darkness,
I clutch my tiny ted!

I've heard some funny noises
From the cupboard in the hall,
I wonder what is in there?
Maybe it's a ghoul!

I'm nearly off to sleep now,
I hear a scary moan,
Hear the scrape of rusty metal
And a terrifying groan . . .

*Emily Cragg (10)*
*Istead Rise Primary School*


## DRAGON

D   ragons are the most feared monsters on the planet.
R   ed fire gushes from their mouth.
A   lone in its dark, gloomy cave.
G   reedy and selfish, the dragon is with its treasure.
O   n a hillside it looks for its next victim.
N   ow there are no dragons left in the world and humans now rule.

*Christopher Treadwell (10)*
*Istead Rise Primary School*

# D-DAY

And when he gets to Heaven,
To Saint Peter he will tell,
One more soldier reporting Sir,
I've served my time in Hell.

When I move up to the ditches,
There's bullets flying everywhere,
I thought about my mission,
To get to the Germans' lair.

But if I take the wrong turn,
I could end up lying on the ground,
That will be my lesson learned
And defeat will be found.

*Michael Walter (10)*
*Istead Rise Primary School*


# MY DADDY

My daddy is strong,
He sits in a chair,
He takes me to bed
And makes my food,
He lets me sit on him,
He goes to bed,
Has a job
And wakes up,
That's my dad!

*Hayley Marden (10)*
*Istead Rise Primary School*

## SNOWBOARDING POEM

S   lushy snow is
N   ot what you want
O   ff piste, on piste
W   ind whistling, wind howling
B   oards riding all
O   ver the slopes making miniature
A   valanches, snow crumbles down the hill
R   apid boards zoom down the piste
D   riving madly, slaloming, people stop at the bottom and stand
I   n the queue waiting to get on the lift
N   udging people and barging people to
G   et to the front of the queue.

***Liam Smith (11)***
*Istead Rise Primary School*


## MONSTER

M   onsters have razor-sharp teeth.
O   n gums with teeth out the side.
N   o soul has passed by that cave.
S   oot, piles of burnt bodies.
T   onnes of shields and swords.
E   very monster should terrorise.
R   ed fire coming out of the cave.

***George Rawlings (9)***
*Istead Rise Primary School*

## CREATURES

Have you ever heard of the 9-headed cat and the 6-legged dog?
I have!
They live in a rainbow cave,
With the bearded fish and the 3-eyed horse.
In the rainbow cave of theirs,
The 9-headed cat and the 3-eyed horse cook a feast,
Fit for the weirdest kind of beast,
While the 6-legged dog and the bearded fish
Wait for their silver and gold plated dish.
When the creatures finished their feast,
They really did look like pot-bellied beasts!
In the morning when the 3-beaked bird squawked
The pot-bellied beasts woke up to dine,
I don't know why they could eat
Another horseshoe or purple beak.
Then the 9-headed cat said,
'Why don't we take a lovely walk through town?'
The other creatures agreed.
They needed a walk after that stomach-filling feast,
You wonder how they walk through town,
Imagine seeing a 9-headed cat, 6-legged dog,
A bearded fish and a 3-eyed horse walking down the street,
I can let you in on a little secret if the creatures don't mind,
They dress up just like you or I!

*Jordan Waterhouse  (11)*
*Istead Rise Primary School*

## POLLUTION

What are we doing to our wonderful Earth?
The world's life is worth
Every penny in the bank
And to God we have to thank.

What are we doing to our ozone layer?
Which is worth as much as a football player,
Polluting the air with our very own gas,
Will we be breathing in a few years?

*Jaime Marsh  (10)*
*Istead Rise Primary School*


## ROCK STARS

You'll find them in the country,
You'll find them in the street,
They are rich and famous,
For one I'd like to meet.
*Bang! Bang! Boom!*
Is what they play on drums,
Music to my ears makes them numb,
*Tring-aling-aling*
Is also what they play,
For I could listen to them every single day!

*Hannah Leeming  (10)*
*Langton Green CP School*

## MY BEST . . .

My best pop star is the wonderful Will Young
Who shines like a star in a dark blue night

My best band are the bouncy Blue
Whose voices melt my heart away

My best friends, Lucy, Ben R, Shannon, Francesca
Who make me laugh and smile every day!

My best water animal is the dolphin
Scooting through the ocean like a Ferrari

My best land animal is the hairy chimpanzee
Who hangs around all day!

My favourite footie team who really are the best is Chelsea!
They're so brilliant, I don't know what to say!

My best colour is the delightful bright green and purple colours
Which are *wicked!*

My best rock chick is the rocking Avril Lavigne
Who rocks the world!

My best boy band are the wonderful Busted
Who are *so* brilliant!

My best mixed-sex band are S Club Juniors
Who are *so* cool!

*Laura Larkin (10)*
*Langton Green CP School*

## POP STARS

This is the poem about the stars, who drive in cars to Mars,
It is a race, a big disgrace, in this case they are all over the place.

In the lead is Will Young, he's the best out of everyone!
Following closely, closely behind are three boys who had not been fed,
These contestants were Busted!

Coming in third place is a girl with a pretty face,
No, it's not A-teens, it's Avril Lavigne!

Coming last is my favourite colour, she's clever 'cause she
thinks, it's Pink!
So the conclusion is finally found, wait, is that the Sugar Babes
going round and round?

*Charlotte Boyd  (10)*
*Langton Green CP School*


## MY ROOM

My room is a space shuttle flying through space,
My room is a very special place,
My room is a monkey swinging tree to tree,
My room is a place where I can shout with glee,
My room is all to do with guess who? *Me!*

My room is a brightly-coloured butterfly flying free,
My room is like a magical dream,
My room has an invisible stream,
My room is all to do with guess who? - *Me!*

*Emma Cobbold  (9)*
*Langton Green CP School*

## A MASTERPIECE STORY

A masterpiece full of colour and glory,
Set about in an old-fashioned story,
A poor old woman stuck in her house,
With just a room and for tea, a mouse.

The night-time came, the wind rustled through,
She curled up tight, she didn't know how to,
With only a blanket on the hard floor,
She woke up all of a sudden and opened the door.

She looked out and with her own eyes,
Saw a colourful dragon, what a surprise
And in a puff of smoke off she went,
Up and up she went, she smelt a scent.

Into the cloud was another land,
Of all the cakes on gold stands,
Drinks and biscuits made into shops,
Massive drinks and bottle tops!

There were candy stick and lollipops by the load,
The dragon said, 'This is the everlasting road!'
So she settled down into a house
And had lots for dinner and not a mouse!

*Alice Endersby  (11)*
**Montbelle Primary School**

## SPECIAL

I had a special hat,
But it was torn by my cat.
I had a special key ring,
But I lost it in Ealing.
I had a special song,
But it seemed to be too long.
I had a special toy,
But it was stolen by a boy.
I had a special fish,
But it looked like a dish.
I had a special cat,
But it got too fat.
I have a special family
And that's the way it's going to be.

*Shannon Foley (10)*
*Montbelle Primary School*


## A WORLD OF MY OWN

If I had a world of my own,
A big mansion would be my home.
I'd get pampered and spoilt all day,
Everything I'd request, I'd have my own way.
My piggy bank would be full of gold
And my age would never grow old.
My garden would be twice the size of a footie ground
And all my friends could come around.
In my house I'd get lost,
It will be so big, but I could afford the cost.
I'd brush my hair with a jewelled-covered comb,
If I had a world of my own.

*Hannah O'Connor-Close (11)*
*Montbelle Primary School*

## THE GARBAGE MONSTER

The garbage monster lives guess where?
He's made of trash and has no hair;
He's black and grey and green and blue,
He's red and brown and yellow too;
He lives deep down inside the bin,
You'd never know, he makes no din;
He quietly sits all through the day,
He sleeps to pass the time away;
Then in the night he goes to see,
What rubbish he can have for tea;
But then one day the ugly lump,
He got taken up to the dump;
He got thrown on a heap of junk,
A heap that stank just like a skunk;
Yet back at home inside the bin,
A tiny monster small and thin;
Was forming there if I'm not wrong,
But not to stay that small for long!

*Miriam Endersby (11)*
*Montbelle Primary School*


## SNOWFLAKE

S  now is falling,
N  o pets outside,
O  ld scarves on the snowmen,
W  hiteness on the grass,
F  rosted car windows,
L  ovely warm homes,
A  ll fingers and toes shaking,
K  nees and elbows creaking,
E  veryone sliding on the ice.

*Charlotte Appleyard (11)*
*Montbelle Primary School*

## WATERFALL

The water drained through stone and brick,
While the shining sun set in the sky,
While the clock went by *tick tick tick*,
As the beautiful butterfly fluttered by.

I wonder why the water is clear,
From rain dripping, the fishes hear,
Sounds of water crashing and tumbling,
While bark on trees always crumbling.

With grass shaking in the air,
When birds with eggs come to care,
The little girls walking along with hoods,
The waterfall completes the picturesque woods.

*Sophie Fenlon (10)*
*Montbelle Primary School*


## THE RAINFOREST

The thick canopy in the sky,
Monkeys who climb the trees,
Beautiful, fluffy birds that fly,
Giant rainforest bees.

Water soaking the muddy ground,
Ferns and giant weeds,
Gently floating with no sound,
Come the rainforest seeds.

Every aspect of the rainforest,
From plants to the animals there,
More flowers than can fit in a florist,
The misty, rainforest glare.

*Louis Hook (11)*
*Montbelle Primary School*

## MAX, THE MAN INVENTOR

Max, the man inventor, built a car that ran out of steam;
The cheapest and the neatest thing that I have ever seen,
But sad to say, it only went a mile or two or ten,
She he had to fill the kettle up and start it all over again.

It went *uhuh* when it started
And *ccchhh* when it stopped
And in-between it went *to-plop, to-plop-to-plop.*

But soon he died from smoking a cigar,
So his wife took over his car,
Everyone was sad,
His funeral went bad.

He was put underground,
All of a sudden he was walking around,
The sun came up and he died,
Now underground he lies.

*Jamie Brocklehurst (11)*
*Montbelle Primary School*


## SUMMERTIME

In the summer sun,
We can have lots of fun,
Swimming in the deep blue sea.

As we play all day,
In our very small bay,
Running and jumping with glee.

As the seagulls swoop,
I play with my hoop,
That's how I want it to be.

*Lucy Wilson (11)*
*Montbelle Primary School*

# A SUMMER'S DAY

It was in July,
I wished I could fly,
The bees flew by,
My brother and I were playing about,
Boy! Can my brother shout,
My dad was doing the barbecue,
My mum was waiting in the Tesco's queue,
We then go out the water,
That definitely made some laughter,
My mum came back,
She hung out the washing quickly on the rack,
The guests then came,
It started to rain,
We were very sad,
My brother was being really bad,
We still had a great day,
The rain then went away.

*Jade Maloney (10)*
**Montbelle Primary School**

## THE DAY

The sun rises on the horizon,
As the rooster calls for morning
And the day begins,
The family has cornflakes for breakfast.

Everybody gets their shoes on,
Dad goes to work
And the children head off for school,
The bell goes and the children go in.

Now it's lunchtime,
Everybody takes a break,
Children burst out with joy,
But then it's time to go back in.

The bell rings, time to go home,
Children pack their bags up,
Families collect their children,
Everybody says 'Goodbye!'

Children finish off homework,
Dinner is cleared,
Everyone gets dressed for bed,
People are going to sleep.

*Sophie Hutton (10)*
**Montbelle Primary School**

## MY LITTLE BROTHER

My little brother, well, what can I say?
I have to play with him nearly every day!
He also thinks he's Spider-Man,
He's the world's biggest fan.
I have to share a room with him, his toys are everywhere.
I have to put my favourite things on a little chair!
He walks around and does his own thing
And when he's in a good mood he starts to sing!
(Don't forget the singing's crazy!)
And when he's not singing, he's being lazy!
But he is only three years old,
One more year and he'll do as he's told.
But after all this madness,
I'll take out all the sadness,
He's the best brother a boy could have.

*Ozay Booth  (10)*
**Montbelle Primary School**

## GREAT FLOATING SNOW

I woke up one morning
And of course started yawning,
I looked out the window,
It was great floating snow.

I looked on the ground,
It didn't make a sound,
My brothers didn't know
About the great floating snow.

I went outside and ran around
And stopped as I saw a huge snow mound,
The time had got late and I was cold.
Then I went in as I got told.

*Danniella Martinez (10)*
*Montbelle Primary School*


## PARENTS

Sit down, stand up straight,
Do your chores and pull your weight.
Comb your hair and do your laces,
Go to school, stop pulling faces.

Get down here, stop climbing trees,
Stop playing with your food and eat your peas.
Do your homework, brush your teeth,
Wash your hands and clean your feet.

Parents always say these things,
Even when the phone rings.
But they don't work in any way,
Because we know parents do the same things every day.

*Layla Moore (10)*
*North Borough School*

## WHAT IS . . . WATER?

Water is the sea
drifting onto the calm beach

Water is the rain
dripping down onto people's houses

Water is ice
sliding down from Heaven

Water is in the human body
travelling round to make you live

Water is snow
banging, striking into our world

Water is a washing machine
spreading all over the clothes

Water is a bath
full of warm gentle water.

*Sam Berry (10)*
*North Borough School*


## COLOURFUL COLOURS

Red is the colour of love at Valentine's
Blue is the colour of the sky which you see every day
Green is the colour of the grass which we play on
Yellow is the colour of the sun which is bright up high
Black is the colour of night which appears when the moon is up
White is the colour of clouds which move and fly around the sky.

*Sijan Gurung (10)*
*North Borough School*

## FLYING COLOURS

Red is for blood in bloody battles.
Blue is for school uniform on silly school days.
Yellow is for the sun that gives us light.
Purple is for my sister's dressing gown.
Green is for crazy teenager's hair.
White is for clouds that go with the sun and sky.
Black is for my dad's teeth, all mouldy and grey.
Grey is for very old people's hair.
Pink is for a girl's bedroom.
Brown if for chocolate that sizzles in your mouth.
Silver is for swords and armour clanging together.
Gold is for rich people's teeth.

***Conor Williams-Cooke  (9)***
**North Borough School**


## WAR

*Twang!* Goes the mighty bow,
*Clang!* Armour hits sword,
There go twenty soldiers straight into the storm.

Blood, gore, fighting,
*War!*

Fighting with your weapons
Or fighting tooth and claw.

Blood, gore, fighting,
*War!*

***Thomas Crickmore  (10)***
**North Borough School**

## MY CAT

My cat is different from other cats,
He likes to be left alone,
I wouldn't stroke him if I were you,
He scratches,
One day he lay beside the fire,
When my baby cousin pulled his tail,
*Scratch!* My cousin was crying,
So from now on, we keep my cat in the cupboard.

*Annabel Farman  (9)*
*North Borough School*


## THE FOODS I HATE!

Mash - it's lumpy.
Cheese - it's milky.
Cabbage - it's watery.
Brussel sprouts - they taste like cabbage.
Pizza - it's got peppers on it.

McDonald's - it's delicious!

*Emily Spice  (9)*
*North Borough School*


## BEDTIME

Bedtime is when you go to sleep
As I weep the night away
As the others sleep in a different land
Asleep every day.

*Penny Baker  (10)*
*North Borough School*

## ALPHABET POEM

A  is for apple
B  is for ball
C  is for castle where people fight
D  is for Daniel, my smelly brother
E  is for elephant
F  is for fire, burning down houses
G  is for garage, where people keep their cars
H  is for hamster
I  is for Ipswich, the rubbish football team
J  is for joke, to make people laugh
K  is for kitten, who plays with you all day
L  is for Liverpool, the best team in the world
M  is for Mum, who cares for me when I'm ill
N  is for nail, that you bang in walls
O  is for orange that you eat
P  is for plant, rotting away
Q  is for queen, sits on a throne
R  is for ramp that you jump
S  is for snow that we love
T  is for tap that drips all day
U  is for umbrella that you hold when it rains
V  is for Vikings who lived long ago
W  is for wind that is strong from behind
X  is for a big kiss
Y  is for yo-yo that you spin
Z  is for zebra, black and white stripes.

*Luke Sharpe (10)*
**North Borough School**

## MY RUBY DOG

In 8 weeks, I'm getting a puppy dog called Ruby,
I'm so excited, I think I'm going to burst.
I run around saying, 'Ruby! Ruby! Ruby!'
7 weeks to go, I've gone Cavalier mad.
My mum said, 'Calm down,' and I replied, 'Woof! Woof! Woof!'
We had dog spaghetti for dinner.
6 weeks to go and we've got the dog stuff ready,
I'm really excited, I've made a dog model already.
5 weeks to go, Ruby is now three weeks old,
I can't wait to see Ruby.
4 weeks to go, I'm practising my dog cuddles,
Just 6 cuddles a day for Ruby, when we get her.
3 weeks to go,
I'll have it in my arms soon.
Cavaliers are lovely.
2 weeks to go and I'm bursting with excitement,
Can't have her yet?
Can't we get her now? We have been arguing over her.
I want to go in my room.
1 week to go, we have planned to put her in Mum's room,
I just can't wait now.
We are on the way to get Ruby
And we are singing a song,
'Ruby! Ruby the dog! We love Ruby the dog!'

***Ben Wright (10)***
**North Borough School**

## RAINBOW

Red is for blood
Orange is for an orange
Yellow is for the sun
Green is for grass
Blue is for the nice bright sky
Indigo is my favourite colour
Violet is for the lovely flowers.

*Rebecca Batt  (9)*
**North Borough School**


## LITTLE TED

There once was a boy called Little Ted
Who would never get out of bed
He would never go to school
Or go to the swimming pool
He would lay there still
Indeed he was very ill
He went to the A&E
And had to wait in casualty
The doctor said, 'There is no cure!'
And Ted fainted on the floor
That was the end of Little Ted
Who would never ever get out of bed.

*Robert Hogwood  (8)*
**Pickhurst Junior School**

## RUBY HAILS AND HER NASTY NAILS

There was a girl called Ruby Hails,
Who used to bite and swallow her nails.
Her favourite nail was the middle one,
She ate it with her index and thumb.
One day she swallowed one that hurt,
Her heart quickened and it tasted like dirt.
She stayed a night in hospital,
Dreading a funeral.
Ruby's parents said, 'That serves you just right
For biting all your nails, alright.'
The pain went buzzing to her head,
That brought her to her latest dread.
Cos on the next day she was dead!
Our little girl called Ruby Hails,
In Heaven did not bite her nails.
For she didn't want to die again,
Since she remembered all the pain.

*Geneviève Zane  (9)*
**Pickhurst Junior School**


## ME AND MY RUNNING

My name is Alex, I'm good at sports,
But when I run, I wear silly shorts,
I find running very hard
But when I run, I run very fast,
I want to do the sand jump,
I know I'm small
But when I'm taller I'll jump higher than them all.

*Alex Read  (8)*
**Pickhurst Junior School**

## THE WRITER OF THIS POEM
*(Based on 'The Writer of This Poem' by Roger McGough)*

The writer of this poem . . .
Is brighter than a light
As adventurous as a cowboy
Yep, that sounds right

As cool as an ice cube
As brave as a knight
As sharp as a sword
And will fight with all his might

As smart as a scientist
As swift as the sea
As sly as a fox
Yeah, that's me.

***Rory Leader  (8)***
**Pickhurst Junior School**


## FRED WITH HIS BED

There was a boy called Fred
Who couldn't get out of bed

He watched some telly
Then had some jelly

He got out of bed
And he said
'Before I get thinner
I want my dinner!'

Sorry bed
I think I'm dead.

***James Martin  (9)***
**Pickhurst Junior School**

## THE PERSON WHO WROTE THIS POEM
*(Based on 'The Writer of This Poem' by Roger McGough)*

The person who wrote this poem . . .
Is taller than a skyscraper
As fast as a racing car
As cheerful as a waiter

As bold as a knight
As fit as an athlete
As sharp as a knife
And always gets a treat

As smooth as a worm
As thin as a piece of wire
As bright as a light
As hot as a fire

The person who wrote this poem . . .
Is as clever as can be
As bold as a rock
And doesn't have a house key, that's me!

*Paul Graham  (9)*
**Pickhurst Junior School**


## ME, JUST ME

There is only one me and that is me
You're you and I'm me
And we are always happy
We like to play and run a very long way
And there is only one me!

*Amelia Taylor  (8)*
**Pickhurst Junior School**

## THE WRITER OF THIS POEM
*(Based on 'The Writer of This Poem' by Roger McGough)*

The writer of this poem . . .
Is the size of a pea,
As fast as the wind,
As strong as the stormy sea.

As smart as a scientist,
As cool as can be,
As handsome as a prince
With footsteps the size of trees.

As lively as a monkey,
As nice as an ice cream on a hot day.
As sharp as a knife,
As useful as the letter 'A'.

*Joe Darbourne (9)*
**Pickhurst Junior School**


## PIPPIN

Pippin's my eccentric cat
I love him catching his rat
He sleeps in my doll's pushchair
If he carries on
He won't have anymore hair
With my cat I love to play
Only a little amount left to say
When he feels tired
At the end of the day
I put him in the pushchair
And stroke him so much
Now just one more thing to say . . .
*I love my cat!*

*Marisa Easterling (8)*
**Pickhurst Junior School**

# A POEM ABOUT A BOY CALLED CHARLIE KANE

A boy called Charlie Kane
He was obsessed with champagne
Charlie Kane was a thin boy
Even his friend was called Cloy
His friend was a name of a champagne bottle.

One day Charlie got very ill
So a doctor called Dr Lottle
Came to his house to check on him
But suddenly Charlie's lungs got very dim
Charlie cried his eyes out.

But the doctor said, 'There's no doubt
His throat is full, and full of champagne'
The doctor said, 'Charlie, you are insane
By drinking all that champagne,'
So he had to have a jelly throat.

*Lauren Storey (8)*
*Pickhurst Junior School*


# SCHOOL ON THE CREEPY SIDE

I was in the school alone,
The people locked me in,
So I slept in the classroom,
I was moving about,
All I could hear was *tick tock*,
The creak of the room,
The water running through the pipes,
I was scared stiff, frightened to death,
That was my night alone at school.

*Alexandra Tinney (9)*
*Pickhurst Junior School*

## PORT DOUGAL HALT

Alas, when Old Doc Beeching came with his axe,
Closing down stations and ripping up tracks,
He pulled down the station but now I tell you
Of the Port Dougal Halt that I, Jacob, once knew.
'Twas on the morning of 1906,
When old Harold Parker was up to his tricks,
The train was on time and all were in good health
And the cleaner was prowling the platform with stealth.
Trains come out and trains come in,
The cleaner's now occupied with the litter bin.
A goods train stops quite suddenly, unloading piles of sacks,
'What'd be in here, blooming diamonds? Nearly broke our backs!'
And as the time did passeth, the trading it did grow
And everything was covered in little flakes of snow.
Sacks, they didn't carry coal, instead they carried salt
And when a minor blizzard came, the traffic it did *halt!*
The engines they did rust away, the wagons they did crumble,
The driver he had nightmares and to the porter he did grumble.
The halt fell into disrepair, the trains they all rushed by,
Besides, a *new* halt had been built where popularity was high.
The platform it was covered with whitewash of some kind
And so when Doc Beeching came, no one seemed to mind!
So that is it, my audience, *but* before you go,
I think that there is something else that you ought to know,
I'm hoping that forever you will treasure in your hearts,
The shed-load full of spanners and the piles of engine parts,
The posters, *Go To Scarborough, 6½d Per Head,*
(Though actually if I were you, I'd got to Hove instead.)
The coal sacks and the milk churns, bicycles and trunks,
Old Geoff, cleaner, ever prowling, decrepit Mrs Monks,
All these things that I knew and that I can find no fault,
In the magic and excitement of old Port Dougal Halt.

*William Wilkes-Wood (10)*
*Pickhurst Junior School*

## A GIRL CALLED MARY

This is a tale of a girl called Mary
Who over the years became very hairy!
Due to an unfortunate habit you see
Of chewing her hair since she was three

Now it must be said, a good child she was not
An absolute horror since she was a tot
She did nothing her parents told her to do
She put cake in her text book and soap in Mum's stew

But the one thing her parents really did hate
Was to be the downfall of poor Mary's fate
She constantly chewed on her hair every day
The penalty of that would make Mary pay

She chewed on her hair even though she was nine
She sucked on her hair in the school dinner line
And as Mary's hair strands became very few
She started chewing her school chum's hair too!

Well, so much of her hair, did poor Mary chew
That she covered her head with a hat called a snoo
Until one fateful day, whilst at the school fair
Her best friend said, 'Mary, you've only one hair!'

It was true, she was right, there was only one hair
But the rest of poor Mary resembled a bear
All the hair she had swallowed, had sprouted you see
All over her body just like a monkey!

So the problem you see is that chewing your hair
Can lead to you looking like a monkey, beware
And you don't want to end up like poor Mary too
Else you may be offered a place at London Park Zoo.

*Olivia Bennett  (9)*
**Pickhurst Junior School**

## GAY PARIS

Gay Paris is the place for me
A lot to do, a lot to see
The Eiffel Tower is a tremendous sight
Lit up spectacularly in the night
Come and see the cathedral of Notra Dame
You might glimpse the hunchback wave his arm
Walk along the Champs Elysees
Sit down and sip a café au lait
Relax and watch the world go by
This is a heavenly place to pass by
Never fear there is always next year
I will definitely come back here.

*Alex Saunders (10)*
*Pickhurst Junior School*


## MYSELF

My name is Charlotte
But my family calls me Parlotte
I am eight -
Isn't that great

I love to go super swimming
But brilliant Brownies
Is always winning

When I am older in my years
There'll be no sign of my fears
I know I will be fine
Because I'll be nine!

*Charlotte Moore (8)*
*Pickhurst Junior School*

## MY BEDROOM

A big fat puffy duvet,
A tape of my school play,
Knickers scattered around the place,
A nursery picture of my face.

Curtains closed and eyes shut,
My mum comes in and says, 'Tut, tut, tut!'
Tickets to the cinema from last week,
A new pair of boots for my feet.

A card that says *I love you, Mummy,*
Because she gave lots of pocket money.
A history book from school
And a costume for the swimming pool.

A birthday card from my best friend,
Receipts from shopping last weekend,
Lots of old books all torn and battered,
Then me lying there totally shattered.

*Kate Samson  (9)*
**Pickhurst Junior School**


## MY FEARS

Ever since I saw a vampire
Programme on TV
I've been scared of the dark
Everyone knows that vampires
Come out at dark
I don't know why I'm scared
My mum thinks I'm pathetic
*I'm scared!*

*Rebecca Powell  (8)*
**Pickhurst Junior School**

## MY MESSY BEDROOM

My bedroom is a messy place,
It's the messiest place on the Earth's face.
Clothes and books on the floor,
Rubbish and toys ever more.
Cobwebs, spiders hanging around,
Mice and rats on the ground,
Bitten blanket, messy bed,
Creepy crawlies on my head.
Wardrobes open, draws are out,
Leaking pens all about,
Ink-stained carpet everywhere,
Come into my room, if you dare.
Duvet cover ripped and torn,
Dusty toys just sitting there,
Dried up plants, dead and weak,
Worthless posters, very cheap.

*Helen Stickling  (10)*
*Pickhurst Junior School*


## ME

My fears, my fears,
Sometimes it's about the dark,
My fears, my fears,
Some bits are what I'm not telling you,
I just don't know why I'm afraid of the dark,
It's just what I didn't expect,
But I will stop my fears,
I just know I will.

*James Kirk  (8)*
*Pickhurst Junior School*

## HOME SWEET HOME

H  ome is my life,
O  n my tiny bed,
M  y big ideas,
E  nding in my head.

S  ounds in my home,
W  hen my mum's on the phone,
E  verybody running around and around,
E  nding when my dad comes in,
T  his place has a special sound.

H  ome to me is a special place,
O  h, I'm glad I have my own space,
M  y home is like a secret hide-out,
E  xciting and great, no doubt.

*Charlotte Kemp  (10)*
*Pickhurst Junior School*


## LILA DIPSTICK WHO SUFFERED FROM LIPSTICK

Meet the girl called Lila Dipstick who was using too much lipstick,
She put on lots of lipstick so she really was a dipstick.
Her poor mouth went stiff and popped in a jiff!
She put on much more and went stiff at the door,
The doctor came round and he suddenly found,
Lila was dead from her mouth to her head.

*Gabriella Robbins  (9)*
*Pickhurst Junior School*

## WAR ISN'T THE ANSWER

I see the guns shooting without any care,
I watch the planes crash falling from the air,
I hear the people screaming for their lives
But war isn't the answer to every fight

I see bombs dropping right before my eyes
I watch the buildings crash and die
I hear only silence except a cry for help
But war isn't the answer to every fight

I see world peace in the future today
I watch and pray to live another day
I hear the bomb coming this way
But one day war won't be the answer to every fight.

*Yazmin Jevons (11)*
*Pickhurst Junior School*


## ALL ABOUT TED

There was a little boy called Ted,
Who never, ever went to bed.

He always had a midnight feast,
With Coke and crisps, the selfish beast.

He never, ever went to school,
Oh yes, he was an unwise fool.

But one bad day he fell asleep,
In the armchair in a heap.

The next day in bed,
He just lay dead!

*Lottie Fletcher (8)*
*Pickhurst Junior School*

## SUNRISE

Sunrise in the world
Australia remains curled
As England wakes
The world remakes
The blue skies, risen again

As breakfast-time nears
The night disappears
From desert to ice
The morning lights
Brighten up our world

As hunger comes to call
Lunchtime comes to all
Japan likes raw fish
While burgers on a dish
Is America's most popular meal

When night sets in
Dinner comes again
Neon lights
Brighten up nights
As another day comes to the world.

*Daniel Mackintosh  (11)*
**Pickhurst Junior School**

## CASTLE BY THE MOUNTAIN

Majestic, colossal, immeasurable,
Regal, royal, grand,
Symbol of power,
Sign of wealth,
Looks over the land.

Place of life,
Place of death,
Place of royal power.
Place of kings,
Place of dukes,
Place of knights and a tower.

But now no knights feast in the hall,
Now no ladies dance in a ball,
Now no sentries guard the gate,
Now no people stay there late.

Never again will battles be fought there,
Never again will people live there,
Never again will people die there,
Never again, never again . . . never again.

*Sam Yoder  (10)*
**Pickhurst Junior School**


## MY BEDROOM

My bedroom is a snug pillow,
My bedroom is a ray of light,
My bedroom is a big teddy bear always to be there,
My bedroom is a land of excitement waiting to be found,
My bedroom is exciting all year round,
My bedroom is an adventure.

*Joanna Davis  (9)*
**Pickhurst Junior School**

## DESTROY

The sky is blue and bright,
The sun is yellow
And the moon is white,
The grass is green,
The earth is brown,
The animals that walk on it make some sound,
There are animals big and small,
There are animals short and tall,
But we are the brainiest of them all.

One day this place that I describe,
Will be destroyed by cars that go by,
Even though we are the brainiest of all,
We will destroy the big and small.

*Lee Miller (11)*
*Pickhurst Junior School*


## UNDER THE SEA

Under the seabed there's more than you think,
The sharks and starfish are having a wink,
Snorkelers are swimming through the sea,
I must admit rather you than me,
Mermaids, octopuses, pearls and fish,
Jellyfish, dolphins and I really do wish,
That all of these animals could be safish,
From those horrible people who like to eat fish.

*Kelly Holdstock (10)*
*Pickhurst Junior School*

## THE DEVIL NAMED WAR!

The great devil roaming the land
Spreading its doom all over the sand,
Bringing grief and despair,
As it crawls everywhere,
Nobody expects it, it is always unplanned

The great devil creeping around
Leaving disaster all over the ground
Its glowing red eyes like fiery garnets
Swallowing whole cities, oh dear, oh darn it
Its mighty feet pounding the ground

The great devil growing on fear
As the scent of disaster is ever growing near
The dark clouds guide it, filled with doom
No need to worry, it'll be gone soon
Always living, never dead
Living in the land of dread!

*Poppy Noot-Davies (11)*
*Pickhurst Junior School*

# RIP

A trapped man in the
Twin Towers who lost
His life and all his power

His family stand at his grave
And weep, but he says
'I am not there, I am asleep'

The frosty wind passes by
As his family stand
At his grave and cry.

*Katy Arthur (11)*
*Pickhurst Junior School*

## FUNKY FOOD FROM AROUND THE WORLD

*Whoosh! Bang! Sizzle! Slip!*
Put that salsa chip in the dip

Fried egg, bacon, baked beans too
Fattening food for me and you

Oh yuck, raw fish
I'll hide some on my cat's dish

Crabs, kebabs, chicken too
Coca-cola, woop-de-doo

Big, juicy burgers, chips galore
Hey, is there anymore?

Spaghetti, meatballs, pizzaroo
It must be Italianoo.

**Ruth Meyerowitz (11)**
**Pickhurst Junior School**


## FANTASY

Fantasy, fantasy, fantasy land,
There is no litter on the beautiful sand,
Without fear of hunters, rhinos wander on the African plain,
Extinct animals are back again,
Rainforests tower high,
There are no chainsaws chopping trees nearby.

World leaders don't even talk of war,
There are no diseases, not even a sore,
No homeless people on the street,
Starving children don't have to wish for meat,
Fish swim happily in the sea,
I wish this was how our world could be.

**Emily Sapsed (10)**
**Pickhurst Junior School**

## CHESSINGTON WORLD OF ADVENTURES

Chessington, one of my favourite places
I see a lot of smiling faces
It has an amazing zoo
I might see a monkey or two

I buy a ticket for all the family
Then you walk in very casually
I read the map to pick the rides
One of them has a very big tide

Head straight for The Vampire
It rises up higher and higher
I speed down with my face in the breeze
Listen to tourists speaking Japanese

Get off feeling very dizzy
Then have a drink of something fizzy
My camera goes *click click click*
I end up feeling very sick

I run up to the water ride
When the splash comes, better hide
I've been soaked and dripping wet
A nice dry towel I should get

Around the corner to Tomblaster
In the cart I must go faster
Shoot a snake with my gun
I'm having a lot of fun

Time to head for the car
Hope it isn't very far
Head down the M25
Park my car in my drive.

*Craig Shankland  (9)*
*Pickhurst Junior School*

## WHISPERS IN THE DARKNESS

Swishing through the walls,
Whistling through my windows,
The whispers of the ghost,
In complete darkness.

Creaking of the dusty floor,
Sneaking on the floor,
The whispers of the ghost,
In complete blackness.

Shadows in the darkness,
Drawing my eye deeper,
The whispers of the ghost,
In complete darkness.

Banging on my door,
Swinging of the curtains,
The whispers of the ghost,
In complete blackness.

There it was!

*Joe Harding (9)*
**Pickhurst Junior School**

## THE WALK THROUGH THE WOODS

It was a freezing, dark night in the woods,
As I walked through the broken trees and brambles,
Up in the trees I could see huge, yellow eyes staring at me,
As If I was a non-existing creature,
I could see tiny, little animals running cautiously away from my
                                          half-hidden feet,
As tiptoeing feet lead me onwards I could feel dead, squashed leaves
Underneath my dirty, battered shoes.
As I march into the centre of the woods,
Huge, mammoth-like trees surround me as if they were a large
                                          troop of soldiers,
As I look up to the dark, starry sky huge fingers block my view,
As I walk to the dark exit of the woods,
I could hear soft feet tiptoeing through the woods,
What could it be?

*Joe Beck (9)*
**Pickhurst Junior School**


## I LIKE AND I HATE

I like the taste of chocolate cake
I like the pretty pattern on a butterfly
I like being snug, cosy and warm in bed
I like my family and my friends

I hate the slime of a slithery snake
I hate being places up high
I hate take-away and times, they get muddled up in my head
I hate the *bills* the mail sends!

*Josephine Rendle (8)*
**Pickhurst Junior School**

## THE WRITER OF THIS POEM
*(Based on 'The Writer of This Poem' by Roger McGough)*

The writer of this poem is . . .
Fitter than an athlete,
As pretty as an angel,
She is someone you would want to meet.

As quick as a lick,
As fast as a flash,
As lovely as my teacher,
As yellow as mash.

As strong as a building,
As kind as can be,
As straight as a needle,
As long as a tree.

*Nicola Stewart (8)*
**Pickhurst Junior School**


## MY HOBBY

Painting pretty shapes
Like a bowl of juicy grapes
Some sweet, some not
Some are cold and not burning hot

Painting pretty cats
Like a multicoloured hat
Some white, some black
Some with a delicious snack

Painting pretty places
Like a country of different faces
Some hot and some cold
Like an enormous, big mould.

*Natasha Deshmukh (8)*
**Pickhurst Junior School**

## THINGS I LIKE AND DON'T LIKE

I am a boy aged eight
Who finds it very difficult to hate
I love the world
And most things in it

I love exhilarating football
I play at Beckenham Spa
I'm very lucky where I live
As I don't have to travel far

I have two little sisters
This is very true
There is Molly who is five
And Poppy who is two

They make me play some girlie games
They even do my hair
They put make-up on my face
They are a funny pair!

*Jack Bridges  (8)*
**Pickhurst Junior School**

## MYSELF

I like jelly
It fits in my belly
Pizza is yummy
In my tummy
I always eat bananas
Wearing blue pyjamas

I love eating fish and chips
I love red rosy me
I love reading Disney stories
And watching them on TV

I'd love to have a fluffy kitten
That could play with me
I'd sing it a soothing song
As it snoozed on my knee.

*Lydia Hamilton  (8)*
**Pickhurst Junior School**

## ALL ABOUT ME

I like chunky chocolate
And things that are sweet
Cuddly animals
And rabbits with big feet

I like to do gymnastics -
Every Sunday I go
I think it's really challenging
To perform and give a show

My spookiest scare
That makes me have a fright
Is the screeching of foxes
In the darkness of night

I hate the clicking of the radiator
And the clacking of the floor
But scariest of all
Is the knocking on the door!

Now you know all about me
I hope you'll be my friend
Our friendship will last forever
And will never, ever end.

*Gemma Martin  (8)*
*Pickhurst Junior School*

## ANIMAL SIMILES

The mole is in its snug, snug home
like a baby in its cot

The woodpecker pecking at the tree
like a hammer banging on a nail

The eel is coiled on the river bank
like a spring in a bed

The eagle looks down from a tree
like some eyes looking about.

*Ryan Stickells  (10)*
*St Katherine's School, Snodland*


## ANIMAL SIMILES

The eagle flying high above
Like an arrow shooting fast.

The rabbit in its burrow
Like a finger in a glove.

The mole in his dark hole
Like a pizza in the oven.

The caterpillar on a leaf
Like a baby on a blanket.

*Stefanie Collyer  (11)*
*St Katherine's School, Snodland*

## MANKY YANKEY

There once was a manky called Yankey
Who was all mean and cranky

He had burling great eyes
And a hat of great size

He came from the planet Slodge
That was all green with sludge

He eats lots of 'glug'
Drinks lots of sludge
That makes him go green
At the knees

He moves with a slither
With a tremble and a shiver.

*Miles McCready  (11)*
*St Katherine's School, Snodland*


## THE LUNAR WEED

The lunar weed
Is a mad wild flower
She eats a woolly sheep
In just one hour

She has four eyes
So she can see
She starts to cry
When she pokes herself in the eye

The lunar weed
Is overgrown and too tall
Once she heard a dog
Her head is like a ball.

*Natalie Bird  (10)*
*St Katherine's School, Snodland*

## THE JELLY BELLY FROM PLANET WOBBLY

The big jelly has a floppy belly,
His favourite food must be jelly,
But on their planet they don't watch telly
And he has a mate on the planet called Smelly.

He has little fuzzy eyes,
But he doesn't wear ties,
He has a zigzag tongue
And their horrible planet is called Sung.

He wiggles around floppy,
But he doesn't go all soppy
And he is *soooo* funny
And another of his mates is called Tommy.

*Jane Bowyer (11)*
*St Katherine's School, Snodland*


## THE SCREAMER

The screamer has a head
That goes a bright red
When he falls down
He goes a dark brown

The things that he eats
Taste nothing like sweets
When he's green
He looks very mean

When he's slimy like a slug
He doesn't like rolling in mud
When he's fizzy
He's very dizzy.

*Craig Curtis (10)*
*St Katherine's School, Snodland*

## MR MONSTROSITY

My name is Mr Monstrosity
I have squidgy arms and I drink tea
Special glass and floppy ears
All the better to see you my dears

I waddle and prance
I know how to dance
I twist and I hover
Ballroom dancing, no bother!

Kids scream and they cry
Be quiet, take a poke in the eye
Monstrosity is the name, better take note
Now off I must trot
To sunbathe on my boat.

*Kirsty Brauninger  (10)*
*St Katherine's School, Snodland*


## MY MEAN MACHINE

My mean machine
Is very green,
It makes sweets,
It likes beats,
Then before you can think,
It will make more and more,
It always likes to rhyme,
All the time.

*Shanee Underdown  (8)*
*St Katherine's School, Snodland*

## MY RAIN POEM

Rain, rain
It's such a pain
Everyone running to the cars
Everyone walking and running so far
People drink beer called Stella
People fighting over their umbrella
People getting in such a big muddle
People splashing in puddles
Rocking boats
Zipped-up coats
Cows gathering up in herds
Soaking wet birds
Children working in their classes
People rubbing their glasses
People dashing
Lights flashing
This was the rainiest day of my life.

*Charlotte Huston  (8)*
*St Katherine's School, Snodland*


## JOSH

There was a boy called Josh
Who thought he was posh
Although he was rich
He fell in a ditch
And that was the end of posh Josh.

*Alice White  (8)*
*St Katherine's School, Snodland*

## MY DOG, TESS

Tess
Is lively, bouncy and fun,
But when she turns rough, the games have begun.

Tess
At night is peaceful and sweet,
After eating her round, juicy meat.

Tess
Can be cute and cheeky,
But also very silly and sneaky.

Tess
With her beady eyes, small and dark
She's big and bold with her yappy bark.

Tess
Can be naughty but under her skin
She's a fun, dumb dog
Who eats from a bin.

*Charlotte Bungay (8)*
*St Katherine's School, Snodland*


## THE LITTLE LOST LAMB

Little lost lamb was walking through the woods,
He stopped a minute and just stood.
He heard a sound and looked around,
Then to his surprise, out whizzed a bee
And said it was me.
Little lost lamb then carried on
Walking through the woods
With the buzzing bee beside him.

*Charlotte Phillips (8)*
*St Katherine's School, Snodland*

## WHEN I . . .

When I wake up, the first thing I see
Is the bright sun shining at me

When I go to school, the first thing I see
Is smiling faces looking at me

When I go home, the first thing I see
Is my mum smiling at me

When I go to bed, the first thing I see
Is the moon shining in at me.

*Rhiannon Smith  (9)*
*St Katherine's School, Snodland*


## THE CAVE

The cave has dark black spiders,
The cave has a horrible, smelly smell about it,
The cave has a cold, damp feeling all around,
The cave has a hole of small, squeaky bats,
The cave gives you a cold, shivery feeling,
The cave has a big, smelly dog,
Belonging to a *breathing dragon*,
With terrible teeth and terrible claws
And an ugly face,
Nobody ever goes in and never comes out.

*Natasha Manning  (8)*
*St Katherine's School, Snodland*

## CARTOON CHARACTERS

Cartoon characters do great shows,
This is how it goes:

Bugs Bunny is a funny thing,
With his big, long, floppy ears.
Everybody knows his name,
He's been around for years!

Tweety Pie, the yellow bird,
Always knows what's best.
Tweety Pie, the yellow bird,
Is better than the rest!

Taz Mania, the whizzy guy
And his floppy, bendy wrists.
Taz Mania, the whizzy guy,
Will drive you round the twist!

Ed, Edd and Eddy, the loopy bunch of boys,
Are always getting into trouble.
Ed, Edd and Eddy, the loopy bunch of boys,
Are always bursting their bubble!

The Cramp twin brothers,
In a hateful world of their own.
The Cramp twin brothers,
Won't leave each other alone!

Dexter in his laboratory,
Work, work, work all day.
Dexter in his laboratory,
Never has time to play!

Daffy Duck with his sticky beak,
Always being nosy
And to apologise to his friends,
He buys them all a posy!

*Jorjia Richards  (10)*
*St Katherine's School, Snodland*

## HAMSTER

H oney is my hamster, happy as can be
O ver and under tunnels as she goes,
N ever stops unless it's day
E very day she sleeps
Y ou don't see her much.

H oney is my hamster, stuffing her cheeks with food
A ll day she snuggles up in bed
M ostly asleep whilst we are awake
S he is noisy in the night
T readmill squeaking as she runs,
E very night while I try to sleep
R unning until morning.

*Danielle Edgar  (10)*
*St Katherine's School, Snodland*


## AN ODE TO TIGGER

Her name is Tigger, she's a special sort of cat,
She's extremely furry and not very fat.
She curls up on my bed at night
And gives all the ghosts and ghouls a fright!

*Ryan Williams  (8)*
*St Katherine's School, Snodland*

## HIPPOPOTAMUS

I stay in the water all day,
I pop out with just my eyes and ears,
Floating in the water I lay,
Resting from dawn to dusk.

My face is very round,
With eyes that are as small as buttons, so small eyes,
I can't even see as far as the sky.

My body is very bulky,
That stubby legs connect,
Don't ever make me mad,
I could do something you might regret.

My skin is extremely smooth,
I swim around in herds,
My voice is so deep and mean,
Like a monster rising from the earth.

*Misty Sheldon  (11)*
*St Katherine's School, Snodland*


## JOSH

There was a boy called Josh
Who was very posh
And he had a toy called Tosh
To get his Tosh
He needed to have lots of dosh.

*Ellis West  (8)*
*St Katherine's School, Snodland*

## AN ARACHNID SPINNING

Small, crawling, black-legged arachnid
Spinning, spinning
Sly, bloodthirsty spider on its web
Waiting, waiting
Never getting tired
Slyly, slyly
Flies beware of its snare
Sticky, sticky
You'll end up in there
Scary, scary
Children keep way
Spinning, spinning
Has a web of silken thread
Mum, Mum
*Splat!*

*Thomas Edwards (11)*
*St Katherine's School, Snodland*


## THE STAR

Last night I saw a little star
Sparkling in the sky
I thought I saw it wave at me
And heard it say goodbye.

*Rebecca Merry (9)*
*St Katherine's School, Snodland*

## THE MEAT LOVER

My fur is like a rug of silk,
My teeth are like icicles,
Hanging in a cave-like mouth,
My flame-like eyes glint in the sunlight,
I have a body of two colours
And my arms are like sledgehammers.

I have a ferocious roar,
A mighty pounce,
Dagger-like claws
And a crushing bite.

I am a meat lover,
Who loves to pounce on prey.
I can crouch beneath grass
And a pounce that pins my prey,
I am very fast,
But also I'm very slow.

What am I?

*Aaron Whatman (10)*
*St Katherine's School, Snodland*


## HORSES

Horses run about
Even jump and shout
They eat hay
Love to play
And gallop on the bay.

*Natalie Bush (9)*
*St Katherine's School, Snodland*

## THE TALIFFE

Taliffe's a beast with
Whopping teeth
Twenty big teeth
With whiskers on his cheeks
He smells like a rat
But doesn't look like one

His teeth are so sharp
He can cut right through bark
As the trees fall down
Everyone is running around

When it has all quietened down
He goes back underground
Sharpening his teeth
With a file underneath
With gunge running down his chin
The dirty big beast sucks it all back
Through his cheeks.

***Aaron Martin (11)***
***St Katherine's School, Snodland***


## NATURE'S ANIMALS

Nature is the better side,
With all sorts of animals.
Big and small,
Fat and thin.
Herbivores and carnivores,
I like them all.

***Joshua Allen (9)***
***St Katherine's School, Snodland***

## THE QUEENESS FROM THE PLANET QUIZ

The queeness' belly
Is like strawberry jelly
And when she is full
She is as round as a ball

She slithers along the street
When drums start to beat
She is a spooddoggy disgrace
With those spots on her face

She enjoys eating jelly
'Cause it slips down her belly
She sits on her seat
Eating her sweets.

*Victoria Sopp  (10)*
*St Katherine's School, Snodland*


## EARS LIKE SATELLITE DISHES

The rabbit bounces along like a pogo-stick
She moves along as silently as the night sky
And has feet like clown shoes but never seems to trip
She has huge ears like satellite dishes, for detecting danger
And rushes to places to hide
She has huge goofy teeth
For nibbling into carrots
She has a soft, furry body
For keeping warm in the cold, grey night
She is very nervous and likes to stick together
With her friends for safety.

*Ross Williamson  (11)*
*St Katherine's School, Snodland*

## STRAY DOGS

Stray dogs are like wolves hunting in packs
Strolling by the moonlit stream
Their teeth as sharp as knives
Moving swiftly, silently through the street at dusk
Ready to strike any movement at all
Afraid in the forest like a baby chinchilla
Running through the forest faster than ever
Its dry fur whipping in the wind
Curling up like sheep's wool
And going to sleep for the night
Silently, softly going to sleep
Walking in the night
Aware of the danger
And moving home from home
All through the year.

*Kris Deal  (10)*
*St Katherine's School, Snodland*


## THE CAT

The cute cat,
Small, cuddly,
Like a little teddy bear,
Like a small baby,
It crawls about,
Like a snake,
As thin as a slug,
As small as an ant,
I love the cat.

*Samantha Moore  (9)*
*St Katherine's School, Snodland*

## My Naughty Degus

My naughty Degus wake up
And immediately knock over the cup

This was full of their food
Which puts them in a bad mood

So now they're gnawing at the cage
Which puts them in a nasty rage

Fighting each other like kangaroos
They tire themselves out and have a snooze

Thankfully they sleep at night
So I can snuggle up tight

*Goodnight!*

**Joseph Bennett (10)**
*St Katherine's School, Snodland*


## The Dog

The spotty dog,
Ferocious, fluffy,
Like an evil dinosaur,
Like a clumsy parrot,
It digs madly,
Like a fast runner,
As big as an elephant,
As jumpy as a monkey,
I love the spotty dog.

**Christopher Lee (9)**
*St Katherine's School, Snodland*

## AN EXCITING DAY

On a sunny day,
In the middle of May,
I went to the beach
And there I was bitten by a bloodsucking leech.
There on the beach,
Was a bottle of wonderful bleach,
I tipped it over.
Most amazed I saw a clover,
What on the beach?
Sitting next to that leech?
Then what happened next?
(Well, apart from someone giving me a text),
Anyway, it gave me an awful fright,
For that bloodsucking leech was completely white.
Then it scuttled off to the sea,
Amazed at how weird I can be.
Well that is me!
This was an amazing sight,
I and a leech had been in a fight,
The leech now rolled,
Extremely cold,
Down those rocks
And onto someone's socks,
Then it rolled down to the sea,
I died with laughter and that is me!
All this happened on a sunny day,
In the middle of May,
On a beach
And all about this leech!
Such an exciting day.

*Kirsty Duncan  (10)*
*St Katherine's School, Snodland*

## THE BEAUTIFUL BUTTERFLY

In the wind it flutters by,
Gracefully flying low, flying high,
Patterned body all colourful and bright,
Showing it off in the day, hiding it up at night,
It lives on leaves and eats them too,
It's as tiny as a mouse, to hide away from you,
When it moves, it hardly makes a sound,
You wouldn't notice it around,
Its body is so silky smooth,
It doesn't knot up when it moves,
Its body is so very dry,
In the wind it flutters by,
Gracefully flying low, flying high,
The very beautiful butterfly.

*Kaye Everhurst  (11)*
*St Katherine's School, Snodland*


## THE CAT

The fierce cat, biting, scratching,
Like a lion,
Like a tiger, it scratches and bites,
Like a terrifying monster,
As fierce as a bear,
As quick as a crocodile,
I am scared of the cat.

*Andrew Chambers  (9)*
*St Katherine's School, Snodland*

# ELEPHANT

Its tusks are pointy like arrows
And help it fight in battles
Its body is as tough as leather
Which crinkles hot in the sun

Its body is as grey as a stone
Which lies on a dusty floor
And it is as big as a house
And also is scared of a mouse

It runs from hunters most of its life
Plodding along with its feet
But often gets caught and shot
Poor, poor elephant, why?

**Callum Johnstone  (11)**
*St Katherine's School, Snodland*


# THE KESTREL

Hanging, poised in the air,
Unsupported and aware,
Of tiny movements down below,
Voles scurrying in the snow,
Rufus head with peering eyes,
Catches completely by surprise,
Any little living things,
Voles on feet and birds on wings.

**Samantha Ripley  (11)**
*St Katherine's School, Snodland*

## HALF HEAD MONSTER

Half head monster
Is quite an impostor,
But when he feels mean,
He turns a great green.

He shrinks himself small,
But he eats till he's full,
He gets too angry,
As he is so hungry.

He has a big axe,
Which looks like wax,
He lives on the planet Mars,
Why doesn't he have a car?

***Christopher Hover  (10)***
**St Katherine's School, Snodland**


## THE BUDGIE

A ferocious budgie
It takes you by surprise
It gives you a nasty bite
Like a furious cheetah
*Beware of him!*
Like a killing monster
It will attack you with surprise
I like the budgie.

***Beau Ripley  (9)***
**St Katherine's School, Snodland**

## THE FRUSTRATED CHEETAH

As the moon goes down,
He gets frustrated,
Nothing to eat,
Not a sound to be heard,
He prowls proudly over the river,
As silent as a mouse,
From a distance gets ready to pounce
On a lonely fox,
Open-mouthed, the bloodthirsty cheetah
Shows huge fangs just like needles,
Digs into an innocent creature,
Tears hungrily away at the flesh,
Enjoys his meal in the middle of the field,
The warm, furry creature sprints to an arched tree,
As he grows tired, he roars like thunder,
The contented, deadly cheetah falls asleep.

*Danielle Balderston  (11)*
*St Katherine's School, Snodland*


## THE DOLL

The dancing, moving doll,
Dancing, singing,
Like a ballet dancer,
Like a princess,
It sings like a bird,
Like dancing on a stage,
As pretty as a princess,
As sparkly as a star,
I love the doll.

*Katy Morgan  (9)*
*St Katherine's School, Snodland*

## BLACK WOLF

B  is for brutalising eyes of blue
L  is for legendary predator, the world's most true
A  is for attitude, keep on running
C  is for clever and very cunning
K  is for killing, tearing and ripping

W is for wolves, wild and wise
O  is for the opening of the wilderness to where it belongs
L  is for loudness as it cries
F  is for its very frightening, fiery eyes.

*Craig Ellis  (11)*
*St Katherine's School, Snodland*


## DOLPHINS

D  own, silently, deep
O  ver the high waves like a rabbit jumping in a meadow
L  aying on his seabed like man after a hard day at work
P  osing in front of the mirror like a super model walking
                                                   down the catwalk
H  iding in the overgrown seaweed like a lion hunting
I  n and out the shimmering fish like a horse sprinting fast
N  ow I hunt for my food like an eagle slowly
S  ilently in the deep dark cave.

*Emma Allchin  (11)*
*St Katherine's School, Snodland*

## THE BUNDLE OF FLUFF

The polar bear is soft and furry,
It has almighty feet.
The polar bear is very playful
And plods in the snow like an elegant dancer.
The polar bear, it's very scared,
But when you get *too* close it's very dangerous.
The polar bear, it's loving and caring,
Its children are so lucky and energetic.
The polar bear, its fur is nice and smooth,
Since I was little I thought it was a bundle of fluff,
Its reactions are quick and is fierce when it wants to be,
A deadly killer, snow-spattered, seal blooded massacre.

*Simone Marner (10)*
*St Katherine's School, Snodland*


## THE GIRAFFE

The tall giraffe,
Spotty, cuddly,
Like a skyscraper,
Like a cuddly toy,
It reaches into the tree,
Like an elephant's trunk,
I like the giraffe.

*Rebecca Keeley (9)*
*St Katherine's School, Snodland*

## CREEPY-CRAWLIES

Scary and hairy
Creepy-crawlies
Scare my mum and brother

Scary and hairy
Creepy-crawlies
Have them running for cover

Scary and hairy
Creepy-crawlies
Never bother me
Unless scary and hairy
Creepy-crawlies
Are swimming in my tea.

*Rosie-Jane King  (8)*
*St Katherine's School, Snodland*


## RAINBOW

The sun is shining in the sky,
All the clouds are going by,
Here comes the rain,
Along past the sun,
A rainbow appears to complete the day.

*Charlotte Sutton  (8)*
*St Katherine's School, Snodland*

## THE THIN FOOTBALLER

The thin footballer,
Fast, small,
Like a tiger,
Like a boxer,
He takes free kicks,
Like Beckham with his golden boots,
As brilliant as the World Cup,
As good as Owen,
I like the thin footballer.

*Michael Stevens  (9)*
*St Katherine's School, Snodland*


## THE FOOTBALLER

Quick, tiny,
Like a cheetah,
Like a tiny slug,
He scores a lot,
Like the World Cup winner,
As good as Michael Owen,
As fast as a bird,
I totally love the footballer.

*Charmaine Tanser  (10)*
*St Katherine's School, Snodland*

## WINTER

W  hirling leaves, golden and brown
I  n the midnight, flying all around
N  othing there, no one there, getting scary, very scary
T  he lightened moon shining down, shadowed ghosts
                                    hiding all around
E  nded lives up above
R  isen from the darkness below.

*Gary Hanson  (10)*
*St Katherine's School, Snodland*


## THE DOLPHIN

D  ashing in the light blue sea
O  ctopus watching him swimming wild and free
L  aying in his bed being lazy
P  osing in the mirror, the dolphin goes
H  urrying up, he wonders off . . . swiftly
I  gnoring his friends, then he
N  icely says sorry to them.

*Nicole Hill  (10)*
*St Katherine's School, Snodland*


## FOOD

One day I went to a lovely shop,
It had a cold ice on a Coca-Cola can,
It was a miracle to be in a shop with a lot of sweets,
I fell to the ground amazed,
I woke up and I paid for the icy cold Coca-Cola.

*Lauren Vidler  (8)*
*St Katherine's School, Snodland*

## Lived The Mysterious Creature

Over the domed hill
Over the whispering trees
Lived an ant with the cooling breeze
Under the dull clouds
Under the frozen lake
Lived the mysterious creature
Back over the domed hills
Back over the whispering trees
Lay a boy dreaming, dreaming, sound asleep.

*Ryan Chatfield  (10)*
*St Katherine's School, Snodland*


## Tigers

T   is for toes
I    is for ignorance
G   is for gatherings around the swaying green tree
E   is for eating and chewing on knobbly knees
R   is for running fast with a roar
S   is for softness as it lays on the floor.

*Jade Pilkington  (10)*
*St Katherine's School, Snodland*


## If I Had A Dream

If I had a dream
I would love to see
Everyone getting along
But dreams don't come true
Or do they?

*Martin Pett  (10)*
*St Katherine's School, Snodland*

## THE PANTHER

The panther lurks in search of prey,
He blends in the darkness ready to pounce,
He darts around chasing the animal,
Until silence, the panther's done its job,
The creature sleeps with joy,
It's not a big deal but tomorrow's going to be a good meal.

*Joe Bottiglieri  (11)*
*St Katherine's School, Snodland*


## DAISIES

Daisies are white, sometimes yellow
Fresh and clean in the gigantic meadow
Suddenly a July shower brings the thunder
Daisies black are scattered asunder,
But out comes sunshine, away goes the rain
Daisies white and yellow smile at us again.

*Jessica Randall  (8)*
*St Katherine's School, Snodland*


## MATHS

My maths is so hard, I can't do it
I never have finished my work,
I always get my answers wrong,
I am one silly boy,
I am the silliest boy in school.

*Ben Chivers  (9)*
*St Katherine's School, Snodland*

## FRIENDS

F riends are great
R egular friends
I ntelligent friends
E xcellent friends
N ew friends
D isco friends
S upersonic friends!

*Sophie Ellis (8)*
**St Katherine's School, Snodland**


## THERE'S A ROCKET IN MY GARDEN

There's a rocket in my garden
I don't know why
Perhaps it just fell out the sky
I won't go near it, in case it goes *bang*
So I'll wait and show the rest of the gang

There's a rocket in my garden
I don't know why
Because it wasn't there when Sam came by
I won't tell Mum, she'll only flap
I won't bother with Dad, he's having a nap

There's a rocket in my garden
I don't know why
I won't tell my sister, she'll only cry
Here comes the dog, blind as a bat
'Watch out, Ky, don't bump into that'

This is the end of my family rhyme
I hope I haven't wasted too much of your time.

*Jack Kairis (11)*
**St Michael's CE Junior School, Maidstone**

# THE BIG MATCH

Twenty-two players in the early morning light,
Ready for a good game, ready for a fight.
The navy and the light blues versus the red and the white,
Ready for a good game, ready for a fight.

The ref is a magpie, black and white down to his knees
And the corner flags flutter with excitement in the breeze.
The colourful spectators twitter like birds in the trees
And the corner flags flutter with excitement in the breeze.

The whistle blows and the crowd roar like water in a flood,
The red and white defence goes sprawling in the mud.
The ball flies, the players jump and bodies crash with a *thud*
And the blues' top striker goes sprawling in the mud.

The ref looks to the linesman then paints to the spot,
The captain of the blues must give it all he's got.
Goalie goes the wrong way and nerves are all forgot,
The captain of the blues gave it all he'd got.

Twenty-two players in the mid-morning light,
Had a really hard game, had a fair fight.
The navy and the light blue, the red and the white,
Had a really good game and the ref got it right.

**Stephen Smith  (10)**
**St Michael's CE Junior School, Maidstone**

## CLASS POEM

In our class there are 27 kids
Some tall
Some small
And some cool
Tall are Scott A, James, Michael
Small are Sherri, Kyle, Joe
And everyone else is cool
17 boys and 10 girls in the class
They all have a ball.

*Mickayla Ratcliffe  (11)*
*St Michael's CE Junior School, Maidstone*


## CHOCOLATE

The milky, smooth, filling taste,
that gives me a craving every day.
It runs through my mind all the time
and makes my tummy go all funny.

In a bar or on a stick,
which one shall I have?
The caramel or the coffee
or the one with sticky, chewy toffee?

*Charlotte Manzi  (11)*
*Shernold School*

## LIPGLOSS

Clear, pink, lilac, blue,
Sparkly, shimmery, shiny too!
Purple, silver, luminous red,
All these colours running through my head!

I do need lipgloss,
But what makes me cross,
Is why they test it on God's living creatures,
They ruin the lovely features.

Last of all, my final say,
Is do not treat animals that way,
Although lipgloss makes you smile,
Animals are not that vile.

*Holly Ladd  (10)*
*Shernold School*


## CHOCOLATE

Hot melted chocolate
Cadbury's and Nestlé
Caramels and Rolos
Yum, yum for my tum
I can suck Rolos all day
And let caramel set into my tongue
Yum, yum for my tum.

*Lydia Jakob-Grant  (11)*
*Shernold School*

## TOWN OF SOUND

Listen to the sound of
Pans clattering, *clish, clash,*
Raindrops falling *splish, splash,*
Hands that are clapping, *clap, clap,*
Pens clicking, *clack, click,*
Board pens screeching, *scratch, screech,*
The person screaming, *help, eek*
The noises I hear are:
*Clish*
*Clash*
*Splish*
*Splash*
*Clap*
*Clip*
*Clack*
*Click*
*Scratch*
*Screech*
*Help*
*Eek*
These are all the sounds
I hear in the town of sound,
The town of sound is in
Your mind if you listen.

*Eleanor Oliver  (10)*
**Shernold School**

## SWEETS

Candy sticks
Lemon drops
Sherbet dips
Fizzy pops
Jelly lips
Baby bops
Yum, yum
They're the tops

Chocolate mice
Um, quite nice
Marshmallows
Pinks and yellows
Gingerbread men
Pound for ten
Strawberry laces
They all give me
Smiley faces!

*Jade Waymouth (11)*
*Shernold School*


## FAMILY

Mum, Dad, sister and brother,
All live in a house with each other,
Birthdays, Christmas, parties galore,
Our families we adore.
Some families don't love each other,
Or they don't have a sister or brother,
Some people don't have hardly any family,
I'm so glad my family loves *me!*

*Grace Rudgard (11)*
*Shernold School*

## NATURE

Nature, nature, wonderful nature!
Squirrel run about,
Pandas, pandas, come out in the
Dark, dark night.

Nature, nature, beautiful nature,
Birds and ducks,
Fly gracefully in the
Blue, blue sky.

Nature, nature, fascinating nature,
Birds, pandas, ducks and squirrels
Are all nature's creatures.

Nature, nature, exciting nature!

*Emily Witney  (8)*
*Shernold School*


## THE SCHOOL BULLY

The school bully came up to me
And punched me in the face,
I ran straight out the room
And started up a chase.
I saw the equipment
And climbed to the top of the slide,
Then I saw the bully coming around
The other side.
The bully soon caught me
And threw me against the tree,
I never want to see another bully in my life,
Because they cause too many accidents,
Worries and strife.

*Isabelle Terry  (8)*
*Shernold School*

## CHRISTMAS

Everybody's happy on Christmas Day
Everybody's happy when they see Santa's sleigh!
Hope you enjoy your ride on your way
I bet you'll say
Hip hip hooray!

I bet he's gone
Now I hope
I get presents filled
With Christmas joy!
Now I'll say
Hip hip hooray!

Now I'm so happy
I'll kiss Mum and me
I really feel Christmassy
I hope you had a lovely Christmas
Like me, Mum and
The Christmas tree!

*Pranav Kasetti (8)*
**Shernold School**


## MY FAMILY

My sister's always playing games,
My brother's always calling me names,
My mum's always doing washing
And my dad's main job is being bossy,
But my family is very special to me,
They're the best that they could ever be.

*Laura Howell (10)*
**Shernold School**

## A FLOWER

A flower, as it starts its life,
Hides beneath the soil and earth.
Sitting there all day long,
Waiting for the sun to come along.
Here it comes, the sun is here,
When all the seeds try to reach up near.

A flower, as it starts to grow,
Needs the rain from the skies to flow.
As the flower stands so tall and proud,
A nasty weed has started to prowl.

As a flower starts to die,
It shrivels up and goes all dry.
It crumples and turns all brown,
This flower no more wears the crown.

*Amy Hartfield (10)*
*Shernold School*


## ANIMALS

Fish swim in the sea
Cats eat up their tea
Dogs go for walks
Parrots learn how to talk
Hamsters run on their wheel
Magpies are ready to steal
Budgies feel soft
Rats live in the loft
Mice live in their hole
Horses look after their foals
Cows make milk
Calves feel like silk.

*Gina Dimascio (8)*
*Shernold School*

## WOODS AREN'T ALWAYS SCARY

Woods aren't always scary,
Even in the dead of night.
The mice should be scared though,
As hawks and owls take flight.

Woods aren't always scary,
Especially in the day.
Flowers all around peep out,
While fluffy bunnies play.

Woods aren't always scary,
Even in a storm,
Watch out for falling trees though
And make sure you keep warm.

Woods aren't always scary,
There are always sunny days,
But watch out for the flesh-eating shadow,
Be cautious, it always pays!

*Rebecca Harris  (11)*
*Shernold School*


## MY DOG

My dog is called Daisy
And she's a bit lazy
She chews her bone
When she's alone
She always barks when we're eating
Especially at the noise of the heating
She always eats the leftovers
And always rolls in clover.

*Eleanor Pile  (8)*
*Shernold School*

## My Dog, Bunny

I have a little dog
And her name is Bunny,
She does lots of tricks
Which we think are really funny.
I take her for walks,
In the woods and park
And all she seems to do
Is run and bark.

She snuggles up tight to me at night,
As she does not like me out of her sight.
She likes it best when she has her tea,
Bunny is the one for me.

*Jenny Cosgrove  (10)*
*Shernold School*


## The Unusual Day

On Friday the 12th
I saw an elf
It was a funny little thing
The way it walked and carried a gold ring
It pulled me along with his eyes shining bright
Up in the sky, up into the sunlight
As we entered the sun's gravity
I closed my eyes and hoped it wasn't reality
But . . . *zoom* into the sun
I thought *I'm a fried bun!*
Luckily the elf was magic
He zapped me home
When I got there, I felt sick
And I needed to be alone.

*Matthew Burton  (8)*
*Shernold School*

## THE CANDY MAN!

Marshmallows, laces, sweet stuff too!
Wonka bar or three or four or two,
I search my cupboard here and there!
Until there on top of the fridge I see it, the candy bar,
I eat and feast on sweets all day.

Till one night I dreamt of candy!
I dreamt of candy nearly all night,
I was in candy land,
I was swinging on liquorice,
I skied with Dip-Dap
And I jumped on marshmallows,
I went up and down really high, honest!
Until I heard a noise,
A magic noise, it came into view,
I was a man,
The candy man!

***Charlotte Wilmore (9)***
***Shernold School***


## MY PET DOG, PRINCE

My pet dog is called Prince
He doesn't look much like a prince
He runs around the garden mad
When it snows he slides down the hill on the sleigh
So his ears pop up!
When he was a puppy
He used to come upstairs and sleep
And sleep on my bed
He sometimes goes around the garden
Sniffing about.

***Christabel Webb (8)***
***Shernold School***

## FOXES

There once was a fox
Who wore green socks

And lived with his
Vixen wife

He lived in a den
With his cub called Ben

And was happy with his
Own little life

He slept all day
And played all night

Under the stars
Was he

He collected food
And took it home

And gave it to
His family.

*Jessica Rogers  (10)*
**Shernold School**


## MONKEY

M  onkey, monkey you haven't got anything
O  n and off that big, yellow swing
N  aughty little monkey in the trees
K  enya, hot Kenya is your home
E  ating long, luscious leaves
Y  ou're naughty wherever you please!

*Nancy Watts  (8)*
**Shernold School**

## MICHAEL OWEN

M ichael Owen scores loads of goals
I  nternational team is England
C  rystal Palace beat them in FA Cup 2-0
H  is club is Liverpool
A  lways in world class
E  ven though they're not that good yet in the Premiership
L  iverpool are my 2$^{nd}$ favourite club

O  wen's my favourite footballer
W  ent to a match Liverpool V Crystal Palace
E  ven better than Ronaldo
N  ever not in world class.

*Tom Cosgrove  (8)*
**Shernold School**


## SPORT

I love all kinds of sport
Horse riding, football, running and more
I'm usually in all of the teams
Cricket, trampolining, anything
I've won awards in all of these
Gold, silver, bronze and trophies
When you play sport with your friends
You never want the fun to end.

*Alice Clarke  (10)*
**Shernold School**

## My School

When I walk round the bend
I see my friend
I walk to school
See the wall (people were scribbling on it)
I went to tell
But they rang the bell
I go to do my test in class
I don't pass! I rush to lunch
But fall out with my bunch
I went to break
My friends had cake.

*Emma Brand  (8)*
*Shernold School*


## Dancing

Dancing makes me come alive,
I like swing, I like to jive,
I like to do dancing with my friends,
I like to dance when it never ends!

I like dancing, it's the best,
I never want to have a rest,
My friends are good at it too,
So could you!

*Ami-Kay Gordon  (8)*
*Shernold School*

## FLUFFY'S THE WORLD'S BEST GUINEA PIG

Fluffy's the world's best guinea pig,
That there could ever be,
As soon as you take one look at him,
I'm sure you'll all agree.

I love him very, very much,
He's the best guinea pig you could meet,
He's very friendly but very shy
And he always likes to eat.

Fluffy's favourite food are carrots,
He's grey and also white,
He has a run to play with in the summer
And a hutch to sleep in at night.

*Lourdes Webb (10)*
*Shernold School*


## THE WOODPECKER

The woodpecker sits in my tree,
*Ratta-tat-tat* goes he.

The woodpecker hops on my lawn,
*Peck, peck, peck* goes he.

The woodpecker flies high in the sky,
*Flap, flap, flap* goes he.

The woodpecker lives in my garden,
Happy, safe and free.

*David Atkins (10)*
*Shernold School*

# WHAT AM I?

I'm the tallest fellow in the zoo,
You look at me, I look at you.

My neck is long,
As are my legs,
I eat green leaves,
I don't lay eggs.

I have a coat of colour tan,
It is unlike that of a man,
I have brown spots which you have not,
Oh by the way, I eat a lot.

With my long neck,
I'm able to peck,
Without straining my neck,
The leaves I can see,
Just for my tea.

You look at me, I look at you,
What do you see when you stand before me?

*Alexandra Browne  (9)*
*Shernold School*


# A CAT'S LIFE

I'm very fat and lazy but also very bright,
I sit there in the sun all day and I go out at night.
I *purr* when I'm happy and scratch when I'm mad,
My owner gives me lots of food but the snacks I catch myself.
My enemy is a dog called Holly who is bigger than me
And tries to chase me up a tree!

*George Edwardes  (10)*
*Shernold School*

## THE VULTURE

At 4 o'clock I get to fly
Totally free, up in the sky,
Not chained to my perch, while people stare,
Looking and pointing, without a care.

Now I fly over them all,
Everyone claps, they scream and call.

I've had enough, I want to be free,
So I fly away where there's no one to watch me,
I fly around up so high,
Seeing rooftops as I pass by.

It's a magical place, exciting and fun,
I'm so pleased with what I've done,
There are so many cars just passing by,
I feel like a boss, the biggest bird in the sky.

I hear voices calling my name,
Oh no, they've come to stop my game,
The falconer and people from the zoo,
Now what am I to do?

I'm cold, hungry and thirsty too,
I'll have to go back to the zoo,
I see my falconer and she's seen me,
Should I go or should I stay free?

*Isabelle Loader (10)*
*Shernold School*

## MY FRIEND

My friend, Libby, is really cool
In the summer we play in the swimming pool
We share our secrets here and there
Some secrets I can't even bear
We care for each other all the time
Libby is a really good friend of mine
I will do anything to stay friends
But not when she drives me round the bend
Sometimes she drives me really mad
And I normally become very sad
But Libby is a really good friend of mine.

*Sophie Howell (8)*
**Shernold School**


## IF I HAD WINGS

I'd lost my friends, it was the end
I'd lost my friends forever,
But if I had wings
I'd fly to the future and beyond,
If I had wings
I'd fly to the past and behind
And there and then I would find my friends again,
But I have no wings, so I live my life in sorrow.

*Rhea Tanna (8)*
**Shernold School**

# THE CONDOR

As I soar across the sky,
Thermals taking me way up high.
Searching in the canyon for my prey,
Hoping I will find some food today.
Then I see something scuttle near a house,
I think it may be a mouse.

Swooping past rocks and cactus,
Chasing after my missing breakfast.
Hurrying, scurrying, chasing, caught,
*What a lucky day,* I thought.
Then I rise back to my nest
And there I stay for some rest.

*Harriet Massie  (10)*
**Shernold School**


# BOYZ

You can get two types of boys,
Some are loving and give you toys,
Others are rough and make lots of noise.

There's this boy I really fancy,
He's a lot bigger than me,
If only he could see,
That I am very pretty.

*Lexy Payne  (10)*
**Shernold School**

# THE HEDGEHOG

I am a brown, spiky hedgehog
I only come out at night
I eat only ants and grubs
I don't really like the light

I am very, very spiky
So please don't touch me
I roll up to defend myself
From animals that eat me

I am a brown, spiky hedgehog
I dig to find ants and grubs
They are both really nice
Especially the yummy grubs.

*Jessica Harris (10)*
*Shernold School*


# HAMSTERS

Hamsters are relatives of gerbils, rats and mice
But unlike the others, they are very nice
They dig long burrows and store food underground
And eat it up in winter when nothing's around

As well as wild hamsters, many are bought as pets
In small wire cages, they are kept
They are cute, cuddly and affectionate too
They drink a bit of water and a little bit of food
They might have a nibble, but never bite
They sleep in the day and come out at night.

*Michaela Savage (9)*
*Shernold School*

## PLAYFUL

I am just a kitten
A playful one at that
All day I play, eat, sleep, scratch
I do not like the snow
It makes my paws cold
But in the summer
I can scratch my claws.

*Rebecca Reardon (9)*
*Shernold School*


## DREAMS AT MIDNIGHT

I had a dream last night,
I dreamt that I was a knight,
I was in a dangerous fight,
I won the fight with all my might.

I dreamt I was a dragon,
A fire-breathing dragon,
I had a fight,
With a big fat knight!

In the morning, I woke up,
I'm holding my teddy tight,
I don't think I want to be a dragon
Or a fighting knight,
I think I'll play with my sister, Megan!

*Rebecca O'Connor (9)*
*Sherwood Park Primary School*

## WILD ANIMALS

Wild animals can growl
And make people yell *yowwwl*,
Wild animals can make you stare
Some are extremely rare
The jaguars growl
The warthog snorts very loud
The giraffe is tall
The squirrel is small
The monkey can make you laugh out loud
But then again, it can make a lot of people laugh in a crowd!

*Karimah Farag (9)*
*Sherwood Park Primary School*


## DREAMS IN THE NIGHT

Every night you dream a million things,
Really, your mind swings,
You dream you're famous,
You dream you're the best,
You dream you're flying,
You dream in your bed,
Whilst you see things in your head.

*Samantha Sweeney (8)*
*Sherwood Park Primary School*

## WEATHER IN ENGLAND

See the rain come splashing and dashing,
The sky never shines like in Brazil but
Brazil is too yellow and mellow.
Then comes the lightning, flashing and
Then trees start crashing.
The sun never shows in England,
The heavens are scowling and
Thunder is growing.
The storm will stay until
Another sad day in England.

*Robert Johnson  (8)*
**Sherwood Park Primary School**


## COLOURS

What is pink?
Maybe a wild sink.
What is green?
The can with Mr Sheen.
What is red?
Maybe a shed.
What is yellow?
Maybe a little fellow.
What is blue?
Haven't got a clue!

*Lucy Ferry  (8)*
**Sherwood Park Primary School**

## A SUMMER POEM

When it's summer, badgers come out,
Rabbits play and mess about,
Squirrels climb all through the trees,
In the lovely summer breeze.

Ducks in the pond go paddling around,
While beavers collect their nest mound,
All the animals are playing together,
All through the summer weather.

It really is a lovely sight,
All through the summer's night,
Summer really is my friend,
I wish summer would never end.

*Taylor Warren (10)*
**Sherwood Park Primary School**


## RONNIE THE RABBIT

Ronnie the rabbit,
Had a big packet,
That was full of carrots,
Because he went to a shop called Harrods!

He opened the packet,
To his surprise,
That the carrots had little eyes.

So he went back to the stop called Harrods,
He said, 'I don't like these carrots,
They have got eyes,
I'd rather have pies!'

*Alexandra Baxter (9)*
**Sherwood Park Primary School**

## DREAMS

I'm laying in my bed
Trying to go sound asleep
My door creaks open
My sister's come in to peep!

I'm roaring on the floor
Like a caged lion
But the next minute
It looks like I'm buyin'!

I'm dancing at my party
To the beat and to the flow
Next moment, I'm shouting
'Hate you all! Gotta go!'

I'm jumpin' like a boxer
I'm punching at the air
Now I'm on all fours
I'm howling like a bear!

I'm rappin' like Eminem
It looks like I want to
I think I'm a footballer
I hear the crowd go *boo!*

**Charlie Elves** **(9)**
**Sherwood Park Primary School**

# GREAT GOLF!

There was a golfer
Who came from far away
He went to the nearest golf course
In the month of May

At the age of thirty-five
He teed off very well
But then his score fell
And he wished he wasn't alive

His score was 85
Which wasn't that bad
But after a while
He got pretty sad

After golf he went to the pub
He had a laugh
Which took the golf off his mind
Then he went home and had a bath.

*Joey Hosier  (9)*
*Sherwood Park Primary School*


# THE WORLD

In the world, trees and fleas,
Plants and grass,
With bees and wasps,
Squirrels and birds,
Flying around and growing fast in the world.

In the world, cars and bars,
With the workmen working hard,
Building stuff where we're not allowed.

*George Poole  (9)*
*Sherwood Park Primary School*

## MILLWALL! MILLWALL!

Millwall are the very best,
Oh yes they're better than the rest,
If we played West Ham, we'd win the game
And everyone would remember our name.

This is the story of Dennis Wise,
He's small, he's hard,
He loves a yellow card,
Dennis Wise! Dennis Wise!

This is the story of Neil Harris,
He once had a chance,
Round players he would dance,
It was like he was in a professional trance.

*Tom Scott (9)*
**Sherwood Park Primary School**


## THE WITCH

There once was a witch
Who lived all alone
And lived in a ditch
With a magic stone

She was very hungry
So she started to munch
She had a bowl of soup
And that was her lunch.

*Ellie Dobell (9)*
**Sherwood Park Primary School**

## SUPER STRIKER

Banging balls in the back of the net
Steve Claridge was his manager's pet
At the age of thirty-six
You'd think he would retire

Dennis Wise is very small
But he doesn't care at all
Playing for Millwall
Playing in every game

Steven Reid has got a hard shot
He takes free kicks a lot
Steven Reid who comes from Ireland
Has a very hard shot.

*George James  (9)*
*Sherwood Park Primary School*


## THE WORLD

The world is here and very near,
Martians have landed with beer,
Gliding down a scary clown,
With a hairy dog on a log.

The clown was big and fat
And had a groovy hat,
The Martians had a rat,
With a big, fat cat.

*Sahidur Rahman  (10)*
*Sherwood Park Primary School*

## WHAT NOISE SCARES YOU IN THE NIGHT?

What's that noise
Crackling over there?
Rattling right here?

The trees scratch
On the windowpanes,
What's that making me shiver?

Could it be a ghost?
I'm dreaming,
I hear this sound again,
But this time it sounds
Like a deadly vampire.

I see red eyes everywhere,
I hope it's my mum
Because she has contact lenses!

And it was, she was going
To turn off the lights.

*Reni Dare (7)*
**Sherwood Park Primary School**


## CHRISTMAS TIME

It's Christmas time
White, thick cream covers the ground
Trees are thinking sparkly thoughts
All the children building snowmen
Parents sitting by the fire
It's snowing, it's snowing!

*Sian Brown (10)*
**Sherwood Park Primary School**

## THE DAY I LEFT

It was a hot day
I went to play
I played basketball with my friends
Before the bell had gone

I went back inside for work
Dad was talking about the World Cup
Brazil is going up
Thomas was reading

The next day I said I was going away
I'm not able to play
My friends were sad
And so was I

So I went away
Thinking of the past
It went so fast
I missed my friends

Then I arrived
I didn't feel alive
Everyone was nice
But I still miss my friends.

***Dominic Robson  (9)***
**Sherwood Park Primary School**

# I LIKE ...

I like the seaside
I like the sea
I like the buckets and spades
I like to be free

I like the seagulls
I like the sunset
I like ice cream
I like my pet

I like my mum
I like my dad
I like him very much
But he makes me mad

I like everything
Everything I love
I love birds and pets
Especially my dove.

*Anuska Sivagnanam  (10)*
*Sherwood Park Primary School*


# I LOVE APPLES

I love apples, they are juicy and red,
I love apples before I go to bed,
They taste lovely and scrummy too,
I have a bowl with lots of apples,
I eat apples all night and day,
They are my favourite fruit,
I love apple juice,
I love apple juice, it makes me happy
*I love apples!*

*Eleanor Tidnam  (8)*
*Sherwood Park Primary School*

## SNOW

How does the snow travel so fast?
Like salt in a bottle sprinkled from the sky
Covers the land in her white blanket
Listening to the wind gliding by
Wiping out our beautiful nature
She tiptoes across the land
So silent, not a sound to be heard
The world is in her hand
The freezing, cold breeze
Tinkles the spine
Held in her world
Not a soul is fine
She cries out loud
Yet no one hears
Sadly, she swiftly goes
Peace is near.

*Gala Chan  (10)*
**Sherwood Park Primary School**


## I LOVE BANANAS

I love bananas, they are my favourite fruit
I could eat them all day and night
If I had a fruit bowl I would fill it with bunches of bananas
For when I get the munchies
They are yellow and bent
And taste heaven sent.

*Joseph Hamilton  (9)*
**Sherwood Park Primary School**

## SNOW IS FALLING

Snow is falling,
The trees are shivering,
Everybody is building the snowy, snowy snowmen,
The snow is a foot deep,
Angels are being made by kids,
But then it has to be the snowballs,
They're getting thrown at the children,
Even at the teachers.
It's covered like it's a white sheet of paper,
Now we've had the fun, it turns into ice,
The smiley faces turn into sad,
But it's not the end,
Look, it's snowing!
So sad faces turn to smiles,
So go have some fun!

*Katie Glendenning (10)*
**Sherwood Park Primary School**


## DANCING

She jumped up like a kangaroo
Whizzing across the floor like a whippet
Wiggle, jump, hop, that's the way to do it

The judges put her down as first
She gets a very big and loud applause
Wiggle, jump, hop, that's the way to do it!

*Rosie Langridge (10)*
**Sherwood Park Primary School**

## THE NATURAL WORLD

The animals of the natural world
Fast asleep, warm and curled
Squirrels burrow a home in a tree
Hiding away, waiting for winter to flee
As Mother Nature sprinkles her magic
The natural world rid of tragic
The little creatures leap on ice
Playing friendly with the mice
Food is stored underground
The scratching makes no sound
The birds and animals sing
And the heart of many ring
As nature sleeps
The world around us, full of peace.

*Alexandra Parnwell (11)*
*Sherwood Park Primary School*


## LUCY'S DOG

You came to me when I was one
Together we had a lot of fun
In my bed I let you sleep
From under the covers you would peep
Everywhere we would go together
In any kind of weather
On holiday you come with me
I took you for a walk by the sea
No better friends could there be
But my dog and me.

*Lucy Walker (7)*
*Sherwood Park Primary School*

## YUMMY, YUMMY, YUMMY

I like food
Yummy, yummy, yummy
Especially when it's in my tummy
Yummy, yummy, yummy
Skips and chips with lots of pips
With gherkins in a burger bun
Yummy, yummy, yummy
I like food
Yummy, yummy, yummy
Especially when it's in my tummy
Yummy, yummy, yummy
Peas and beans with lots of cheese
Yummy, yummy, yummy for my tummy
That's what I like for dinner.

*Iain Kemp  (8)*
**Sherwood Park Primary School**


## FOOD

My favourite food is Skips and chips
But I also like apple pips
When I go to the food store
My tummy starts to rumble
Then I see the sweets, yummy yummy
I think it's scrummy yummy!
I love food, yummy yummy
Especially when it's in my tummy, yummy!

*Sophie Gardener  (8)*
**Sherwood Park Primary School**

## RISE AND SHINE

My mum's waking, no mistaking,
She can't be wasting any time dating,
She's also dancing, not even prancing.

She's getting her shoes,
Got to get a move on,
No time to waste now,
We have to taste now.

Making me look smart,
As quick as a dart now,
My sister too slow,
But we've got to go, go.

I thought it was boring,
I am snoring,
I want to go home,
It's too late now.

*Tristan Wallace (10)*
**Sherwood Park Primary School**


## TWO GOLDFISH

I saw two beautiful goldfish
Swimming around in a tank
I said to Mum, 'Please let's buy them.'
So Mum said, 'Okay.'
So we went to the bank
To buy the tank
And they bought the fish with the tank.

*Emma Townsend (7)*
**Sherwood Park Primary School**

## MY RECORDER

My recorder goes *toot, toot, toot*
Just like a *flute, flute, flute*
When I play a song
All my friends play along
My recorder goes *toot, toot, toot*
Just like a *flute, flute, flute*

My recorder goes *toot, toot, toot*
Just like a *flute, flute, flute*
When I play pease pudding hot
Everyone thinks it's pease puddy pot
My recorder goes *toot, toot, toot*
Just like a *flute, flute, flute.*

***Sophie Landick  (8)***
**Sherwood Park Primary School**


## A SPECIAL FISH

I saw two beautiful goldfish
Swimming around in a tank
I asked my mum, 'Can we buy them?'
'OK,' said my mum, 'let's go off to the bank'

We paid for the beautiful goldfish
And carried them home in a bag

I called my fishes Hig and Hay
I gave them a home in a tank.

***Lauren Hopkinson  (8)***
**Sherwood Park Primary School**

## THE MAGIC FOOTBALL

There was a magic football
Which made you win games
It would fly through the air
And it belongs to James

James took care of it
And kept it in his bag
He kept it all a secret
And he never told a soul
He kept winning by scoring
All the goals

James was really happy
Later on that week
James had the flu
He felt a bit weak.

*Sophie Harrison (9)*
*Sherwood Park Primary School*


## BURGERS AND CHIPS

I like
Chips
They're
Yummy
And
Scrummy
And they're
Nice for
My
Tummy.

*Jake Tucker (8)*
*Sherwood Park Primary School*

## Naughty Boy, Ben

There was once a naughty boy
His name was Ben Ladee,
Once at school he was really bad,
'Cause he beat up Leonard Dasee.

Leonard had to go to the hospital
Because he had broken his leg.
Ben got a two-hour detention
And got slapped by Leonard's mum, Meg.

He got told off by Mr Michaels,
The headmaster of the school.
Ben's parents had to come in,
But they didn't care what he did at all.

They told him he was just like them,
They were school bullies too.
They say they don't care what he does,
'Cause we will always love you!

*Emily Middleton (10)*
**Sherwood Park Primary School**


## Snow!

Playing in the snow, all day long
Throwing snowballs at Tom
The snow soft like a blanket of silk
Still snowing all day long, children building snowmen

Children running like cheetahs in a battle
And stomping in a very big rattle
Jumping up and down around
With a loud sound.

*Sam Beach (11)*
**Sherwood Park Primary School**

# WE ARE FAMILY

My mum is always caring,
She likes to hang around,
She is always there for me,
But she hates to hear a sound.

My dad has a spiky beard,
But he acts just like a boy,
He loves to go go-karting,
But he's cuddly like a toy.

My brother's nickname is Elvis,
A bog brush he has for hair,
Sometimes I like to annoy him
And it makes him go in despair.

My rabbit has the cutest face
And her name is Tash,
She lives with a rabbit, Sumi
And his coat is as black as ash.

My cat is a tortoise shell type,
She's scared of all our fish,
Her Whiskas cat food reeks,
As it's served up on a dish.

We're what makes a family,
We stick together like glue,
We hardly ever fall out
And we try not to argue.

*Kristy Blackwell (10)*
*Sherwood Park Primary School*

## MY DAD'S SOCKS

My dad's socks are as smelly as can be
When I smell them, oh dear me
And where does he put them?
He puts them under pillows
And with handkerchiefs and all
His trousers, his pants
And that is all
For breakfast as he comes down the stairs
His socks smell as bad as a cow pat
As the smell comes down the hall
My brother falls to the ground
And my mum says, 'Change your socks!'
My dad's socks are smelly
And that is all.

*Lordi Tickell  (8)*
**Sherwood Park Primary School**


## SNOW

Snow is falling like a waterfall
Snowman is getting higher
The little pond is frozen with ice
Snowballs in war fire

Snow as white as white could be
As soft as the smoothest silk
Snow is melting, winter's over
Spring is nearly here.

*Richard Taylor  (10)*
**Sherwood Park Primary School**

## CATS

Sneaking along the floor,
Tail swishing, whiskers tickling,
Pouncing for its prey,
Like a tiger in a jungle.

Through the night,
Eyes gleaming with green,
As trees shaking,
Two cats go in for a fight.

Sitting on the owner's lap,
Twisting and turning on the ground,
Leaping through the air like a bird,
Chasing its playful friend.

Curled up in a blanket,
Purring as it sleeps,
Dreaming of mice and birds,
The cat sleeps peacefully alone.

Stroking its soft, gentle fur,
Whiskers tickling against the palm of your hand,
Smoothly across your face,
The cat's beautiful and calm.

***Charlotte Campbell (11)***
**Sherwood Park Primary School**

## SNOW, ICE AND FROST

Snow has fallen all around
It's like a blanket of thin silk
Powder that's as white as whitener
Flakes are patterns in the sky

The blanket of silk has melted away
All that's left is ice
This slippery substance cannot move
It lies there now, it lies there tomorrow

Once again the slippery substance has melted away
There is nothing left but a deep frost that covers the grass
It is like sugar on a fairy cake
It's getting warmer as the sun draws near

The frost has gone
Like magic it is
Where has it gone?
That's the mystery of winter
Never to be solved.

*Ricky Lawrence (11)*
*Sherwood Park Primary School*


## SNOW

Snow is white, as white as milk
Snow is soft, as soft as silk
There is a purpose for soft, round sphere
To throw at people and people far from here
Snowballs are fired like arrows in battle
Because the snow is harder than cattle.

*George Cocks (10)*
*Sherwood Park Primary School*

## OUR DOG

Bone-cruncher
Car-chaser
Hole-digger
Cat-fighter
Ankle-biter
Sharp-toother
Fast-mover
Daytime-creeper
Moaning-weeper
Tail-wagger
Tooth-dagger
Floor-sitter
Carpet-layer
Children-lover
Ball-player
Mad-runner
Stick-fetcher
Meat-eater
Man's-best-friend.

*Colby Ramsey (10)*
**Sherwood Park Primary School**


## MY BABY BROTHER

When I look at my baby brother
He makes me happy
When I'm on the floor, he tickles me
He puts his tongue out at me.

*Reece Dunlevy (8)*
**Sherwood Park Primary School**

## MOONLIGHT!

The night-time awaits
As the sun dies down
The cat dances
And watches the flowers go brown
The sun goes down
And the moon goes up
He lights up the sky
Birds fly high
The people are sleeping
And the animals are creeping
Goodnight, sleep tight.

*Catherine Webster (11)*
**Sherwood Park Primary School**


## FLIES

Flies are very fast
Whizzing through the air
They are always on your toys
Then they go away
And land on your food
But they never go, so *splat*
Went Billy Batchelor
With his brand new spatula.

*Billy Batchelor (8)*
**Sherwood Park Primary School**

# MY CAT

Tail-flicker
Mouse-licker
Wet-kisser
Deep-sleeper
Night-creeper
Mouse-eater
Thin-feeter
Moon-howler
Bad-growler
Fur-licker
Bad-tricker.

***Penny Cumbers  (10)***
**Sherwood Park Primary School**

# BAT KENNING

Dark-lover
Light-hater
People-scarer
Flying-time
Big-rat
Many-types
Fruit-eater
Hanging-sleep
Cave-dweller
Flying-bat.

***Billy Rixon  (10)***
**Sherwood Park Primary School**

## THE CLASSROOM

Another new lesson, history I suppose,
Now it's about Victorian clothes,
The teacher is like a whisper, like the wind,
Hours pass,
But it's only minutes in my class,
Children chatter,
Tables are a-clatter,
I daydream, then listen again and again,
Pencils patter like the rain,
Everything is a jumble, we are all busy,
All my friends are in a tizzy,
Ten more minutes till the end,
But soon a lesson will start again
And I will work again and again.

*Hannah Nugent (10)*
*Sherwood Park Primary School*


## MY CRAZY COUSIN

My crazy cousin, Benji, is really very mad
Yet sometimes he's naughty and bad
He plays with ice and makes silly shapes
He scares my grandma for goodness sake
He loves to dance and dance all night
He sometimes likes to have a fight
Sometimes he's very sweet and likes to smell feet
Sometimes he's mad and nice
That's Benji for you.

*Jazmine Moss (9)*
*Sherwood Park Primary School*

## NIGHTMARES!

I'm terrified of nightmares and I'm scared of sleep at night,
I clutch my bedclothes with fear and wake up shaking with fright!
Last night I dreamt of dragons, breathing fire in my face,
But then I met green aliens, slimy and from space!
I sometimes meet huge monsters, like huge gloops of jellies,
Ferocious, huge giants that want me in their bellies!
I stumble around in circles and into caves of bats,
I see huge, hulking shadows, much larger than my cats!
Inside the dark forests, trees are frowning and moaning
And through the night air, the awful sounds of groaning!
The old witch is cackling and the cauldron groans,
Her potion chuckles sending chills through my bones!
I'm terrified of nightmares and I'm scared of sleep at night,
I clutch my bedclothes with fear and wake up shaking with fright!

*Samantha Johnson (11)*
**Sherwood Park Primary School**


## I SAW ...

I saw some light
and I felt bright.

I saw a rat
and I fell on a big, fat mat.

I saw a ghost
and I began to boast.

I went in the bar
and I said *hello* to a car

I saw a clock, *tick, tick*
I think I'm going to be sick!

*Shreel Patel (8)*
**Sherwood Park Primary School**

## THE HORRID TEACHER

She shouts like a preacher,
She is as quick as a cheetah.
She is sly as a fox,
She is as flat as a cardboard box.
She likes silence,
She tames us like lions!
She treats us like litter,
She is ever so bitter.
She never smiles,
She gives us homework! Piles and piles.
She is my horrid teacher,
She is nasty Miss Leacher!

*Pinar Coskun (11)*
**Sherwood Park Primary School**


## SNOW

A cold blanket of snow falls from the sky,
Making the floor look like white milk,
Children scattering from their home,
Children feel as if they're on a cloud,
Soon the sun comes up from his bed,
Children try to play but they can't,
It's time to say goodbye to him again.

*Jack Quarrington (10)*
**Sherwood Park Primary School**

## SNOW

Playing in the snow, kicking the ball
Throw snowballs, everybody's having fun
The snow covers the playground
You get hit by a snowball
Snowman's starting to melt
The snow, soft as silk
Stays snowing all day
Playing in the snow all day long
All the children going crazy
Everybody having fun.

*Alex Roberts (10)*
*Sherwood Park Primary School*


## SNOW

It is snowing,
Wind is blowing,
A cushion of snow lies on the ground,
Children building snowmen all around.

Tall or short,
Fat or thin,
The sizes are very different,
But not the features.

*Amrita Chana (10)*
*Sherwood Park Primary School*

## THE RIVER

The river making a trickling noise as it's flowing past,
The fish gliding through it very fast,
The sun is shining, the fields are green,
After summer, it will be autumn, where the leaves are a crusty
                                    brown that I have seen.

The old, tall tree that the children climb,
The birds sing a beautiful chime,
The flowers are very pretty colours
And on the other side of the river, there are many others.

*Victoria Holland (10)*
*Sherwood Park Primary School*


## FAIRIES

Fairies dance, fairies play
Only in the month of May

Fairies eat with a spoon
Only in the month of June

Fairies sit, fairies fly
Only in the month of July

Fairies swing, fairies sway
Every single day.

*Jessica Wilson (9)*
*Sherwood Park Primary School*

## ALL IN ONE DAY

Spring grows just like a baby
Branches wave as they see the flowers
The wind whistles, the leaves rustle
As they make a song
The sun comes up and smiles at us all
It's time to get up and go to school
The birds come up to you and tweet their song
They repeat over and over
The car is a person talking to the road
'Sorry, am I hurting you?'
The darkness is coming, the cold has come
Children are not playing, they've all gone home
Children are sleeping
Nightmares and dreams have come
Morning is near
You've just got to wake up.

*Katie Ryan (11)*
*Sherwood Park Primary School*


## SPRING

The leaves and flowers outside in spring,
Are full of lovely smells and things,
Like lavender, when waking in the morning,
When the sun shines down upon you yawning!

*Matthew Allen (10)*
*Sherwood Park Primary School*

## DEAR DIARY

Today my dog ate my homework,
So I had to tell my teacher,
Then I had to do some more work,
Today I saw a bird who was a chirper,
Today my cat turned on the TV!
My mum wouldn't believe me,
But I said, 'I'm sorry.'
So I took a chocolate for my tummy,
Today my friend said, 'Hello, goodbye, I'm late, late, late!'
So I went to the park on my own,
I wanted to know why he was late,
So then my fish put water on the phone,
My mum said, 'It was me!'
So she told me to go to bed,
'Lights out!'
'Oh, but Mum . . . '

*Tierney Smith  (10)*
*Sherwood Park Primary School*


## SPRING

I like the sound of birds
And the sun shining
I don't like the rain or spiders
I like Harry Potter, summer
And swimming in the sea
I don't like cold, wet, horrid days.

*Anneka Harley  (9)*
*Sherwood Park Primary School*

## SNOW TIME!

The cold snow is like a warm white blanket
It covers all our land
The snow trickles down people's backs
As people are wrapped up so warm
People's footprints imprint in the snow as they walk
Steam comes out of people's mouths as they talk
Children playing on sleighs
Down the hills they go!
The snow is all around
Making us be full of joy
Children playing nicely on their sleighs
Down the hills they go!

*Shelley Cousins  (11)*
**Sherwood Park Primary School**


## RAIN IS DANCING IN THE SKY

Rain is dancing in the sky
Falling down into your eye
When the sun shines, the waters gleam
Rising up out of the stream

A rainbow is a great big arch
I first saw one, a day in March
I like the way a rainbow bends
A pot of gold at both ends.

*Toby Jones  (10)*
**Sherwood Park Primary School**

# ME AND MY FRIENDS!

We are best friends,
Together we fly,
We are four stars,
Twinkling in the sky.

Firstly, there's Samantha,
Always so merry and bright,
Her games are always fun,
She never gives you a fright!

Secondly, there's Paige,
Always good for a laugh,
She guides you the right way,
When you're acting daft!

Thirdly, there is Hannah,
Sensible and kind,
You giggle when she is around,
She never twists your mind!

Lastly, there is me,
Happy as a flower,
I'll talk so that you're never bored,
Hour after hour!

So now you know my friends,
They're better than the rest,
They will always be,
Always be the best!

***Courtney Stone  (10)***
**Sherwood Park Primary School**

## MIDNIGHT EXPRESS

The night-time express is coming
The powerful sun's rays has met its match
The moon guides the way
We can hear the night express drumming

As the sun goes down, it fights for its survival
He's had his time now, night falls
As the moon rises
To the eye of man it sees quite delightful

All aboard the train to Dream Street
On the train we hear a tune beat
We start to sleep now
Capture this moment and don't let it go now.

*Robin Martin (10)*
*Sherwood Park Primary School*


## MY FAMILY

My family is special,
Families are kind,
They always give me love
And never twist my mind,
My family is my guardian angel,
They always guard me day by day
And in a very special way,
They are my special friends,
Our love for each other will surely never end.

*Emma Longbon (10)*
*Sherwood Park Primary School*

## MONSTER!

In the floorboards and in the street
There is something you won't want to meet
It's as big as a bull, it's also hairy
To little children it's very scary
It comes out from under the bed at night
Giving the children a terrible fright
When it gets them, they never come back
It eats them up for a light snack.

*Bradley Bodfield  (11)*
*Sherwood Park Primary School*


## SNOW

Snow is a white blanket that covers the world
It looks like icing that covers a cake
The snow is fun and exciting
Children having snowball fights
And lots of people having a fright
It covers our car
So we can't go very far.

*Casey Saunders  (10)*
*Sherwood Park Primary School*


## THE WOLF

The moonlight reflects upon the lake
The wolf stares at the moon and howls
And the echo of howls wakes up the street
And soon the sun will come up and smile.

*Anthony Lee  (11)*
*Sherwood Park Primary School*

## FUNFAIR KENNING

Children screaming
Parents laughing
Eating ice cream
Having fun
Funny mirrors
Many games
Silly clowns
Mini races
Scary roller coaster
Haunted house
Sticky candyfloss
Wonderful fair.

*Nima Uddin  (11)*
**Sherwood Park Primary School**


## A SNOW POEM

Snow is a blanket that covers the ground
Like icing sugar, bits of snow coming from the sky
Snowflakes are biscuits with icing on
Children open the door
They fall to the floor
And throw snow at the car
But it doesn't get very far.

*George Oschman  (10)*
**Sherwood Park Primary School**

## CAT KENNING

Fur licker
Mad runner
Wild climber
Fish eater
Mad scratcher
Bird catcher
Milk drinker
Tail wagger.

*Samiur Choudhury  (10)*
**Sherwood Park Primary School**


## DOGS

Dogs are like cuddly toys
Except the naughty ones
If you are in trouble they will care
They can be very funny
Even when they chase a bunny
They can be very fierce
But most of them can be very kind
Dogs can run like a lion
Thinking they are the fastest.

*Demi Hayes  (11)*
**Sherwood Park Primary School**

## MY KITTEN

She's in the house
Can you guess what it is?
She is all black
And she doesn't scratch
She runs really fast
She's four months old
She has long whiskers
And sharp claws
She has a tail
And she is a cat.

*Kellie Jackman-Smith  (10)*
*Sherwood Park Primary School*


## SNOW

Now snow is falling
Hurry back, let's play in it!
Let's get our gear
But first let's cheer
Wake up Mum and Dad
Boy, they won't be sad
Let's build a snowman
Yeah, yeah
And put a hat on
Don't forget the carrot.

*Ben Cullum  (10)*
*Sherwood Park Primary School*

# THE RAIN

I see the rainclouds in the sky,
Dark and grey and way up high.

I hear the thunder start to roar
And then the rain begins to pour.

I feel the rain run down my face,
I really must speed up my pace.

I taste the rain from up above,
A flavour which I really love.

I smell the grass which smells so sweet,
Underneath my two wet feet.

The rain has stopped, the sun is out,
'Oh look, a rainbow!' I do shout.

*Michael Heming (9)*
*Sherwood Park Primary School*


# SNOW

Snow is coming down in trios
From the winter sky
Coming down
From way up high
It's glistening in the darkness
Like white rain
Snow is great to some people
To others it's a pain
Some people would even prefer rain.

*James Bilewicz (9)*
*Sherwood Park Primary School*

## LIGHTNING

One dark night there was some lightning,
It was so very frightening.

I stared at the lightning's shine,
But I felt a shiver down my spine.

I ran for my mum's door,
There was mess on the floor.

I jumped in bed with my mum and dad,
I was feeling very sad.

Then it wasn't scary and it did not frighten me,
Then it came again and my thoughts got over it.

That was when I was small,
Now I am tall.

*Dex Cook  (10)*
**Sherwood Park Primary School**


## COLOURS OF THE RAINBOW

Red is for strawberry
Yellow is for sunshine
Orange is for an orange
Green is for grass
Indigo is for a plum
Violet is for a flower
Blue is for the sky.

*Crystal Wynn  (9)*
**Sherwood Park Primary School**

## I LIKE EVERYTHING

I like blue
I like pink
Who made everything?
The sky is blue
The sun is yellow
Who made everything?
I like dogs
I like cats
Who made everything
I like snow
I like sun
Who made everything
I like school
I like home
And God made everything.

*Thepaah Sivagnanam (8)*
**Sherwood Park Primary School**


## SPRINGTIME

Springtime, the flowers start to grow,
Lambs and sheep start to play,
Trees grow, blossom by night and day,
Kids playing outside,
The weather is getting warmer,
Ice creams all around.

*Thomas Bailey (9)*
**Sherwood Park Primary School**

## ANIMALS

I like animals
I like animals
I like the buzzy bees
Flying in the trees
I like animals
I like animals
I like the furry dogs
Running on logs
I like animals
I like animals
I like the wet fish
Eating from a dish
I like animals
I like animals
I like the silly monkeys
Sitting on donkeys
I like animals
I like animals
I like the slimy octopus
Swimming in the water
I like animals
I like animals
I like the floppy rabbits
They have lots of habits
I like animals
I like animals
I like the hairy gorillas
Climbing trees in the jungle
I like animals.

*Daisy Edwards (8)*
**Sherwood Park Primary School**

## COLOURS

What is pink? A pig is pink
What is blue? The sky is blue
What is white? The clouds are white
What is green? A grasshopper is green
What is red? A rose is red
What is yellow? A daffodil is yellow
What is gold? My necklace is gold
What is silver? My pencil is silver
What is black? My school bag is black
What is brown? My hair is brown.

*Samantha Underwood (8)*
*Sherwood Park Primary School*


## THE WINTER'S SNOW

Tumbles down with pride
And shows a blanket to the ground
Icing sugar covers the world's cake
As it twinkles down from the sky
As white as milk scattered along
*Crunch! Crunch!*
As you walk upon it
Snowballs being thrown across the road.

*Pembe Cesuroglu (11)*
*Sherwood Park Primary School*

## UNTITLED

I like football because it is fun
I like snow, as white and cold as bright milk
I like cakes, as soft as sponge
I like summer because you can get your swimming pool out
I like snow because I can throw snowballs at my friends
I like my computer because I can play games on it, like cards
I like my friends because they play with me a lot at play time
I like my dinner and my birthdays because you get nice toys to
                                                    play with
I like my cats and rabbits because they are soft and cuddly.

*Sophie Laming  (10)*
*Sherwood Park Primary School*


## A MAGICAL FLYING POLAR BEAR

In the cold, crispy Antarctica
In a thick, misty blizzard
A baby polar bear whimpers for its mother
It is a small baby polar bear
With fur as soft as a cushion
As cute as a guinea pig
Its wings are as strong as a lion
Fly little one, fly
Use your powerful wings
Flap, flap like you never have before.

*Ryan O'Donnell  (10)*
*Sherwood Park Primary School*

## WHAT IS THIS COLOUR?

What is pink?
A pig is pink
It loves to wink
What is blue?
The sky is blue
It gives you a clue
What is green?
The grass is green
The creatures are mean
What is red?
A strawberry is red
Louise said.

*Rachel Temple  (8)*
**Sherwood Park Primary School**


## FAIRIES

Fairies sleep, fairies weep
Only in the middle of May

Fairies swing, fairies sway
Every single day

Fairies read, fairies write
Only in the month of July.

*Charley Bland  (10)*
**Sherwood Park Primary School**

## COLOURS

What is blue? The sky is blue
That shines in the light
What is green? The grass is green
That shines in the night
What is violet? A flower is violet
That shines in the blazing sunset
What is red? The roses are red
That go with the sun
What is pink? A rose is pink
By a fountain's brink
What is yellow? The sun is yellow
That makes the day better.

*Daniel Umney  (8)*
**Sherwood Park Primary School**


## MY CATS

My cats sleep on the TV, they jump up and down
My cats jump on my mum's lap and pad on her chest
We get a piece of string and drag it and they follow it
When I sit on a chair, I get a piece of string and pull it
My cats jump

One's called Kat
Her favourite food is chicken
Darcey eats more than Kat
Darcey is greedy
He's grown bigger
Since we got him.

*Thomas Harbor  (8)*
**Sherwood Park Primary School**

## My Dog Called Timmy

My dog called Timmy
Is very pretty,
He barks a lot
And runs about.
He sleeps on my feet
And wriggles on my feet,
He trips me up and likes tug of war games,
I give him treats when he is good,
I smack him hard when he is bad!
He is sometimes a bit smelly
And he is as cuddly as a teddy,
I love my dog called Timmy.

*Esther Finch (8)*
*Sherwood Park Primary School*


## Dogs

My dogs are the best but sometimes they make a mess
They are cuddly like a teddy but sometimes they are smelly
They are cute and small but I'm very tall
They've got little tails that wiggle all day
They play-fight too but most of all, I love them all.

*Jack Presland (9)*
*Sherwood Park Primary School*

## MY DOG, PRINCE

My dog, Prince, was a lovely dog,
He runs everywhere,
But when he was put to sleep,
It was hard to bear,
I wish he would come back,
But now he's gone,
Somehow everything's gone wrong,
When he was a puppy,
He was so cute,
But of course he didn't wear a suit,
I was going to call him Vince,
But lucky me, I called him Prince!

*Georgia Francis (9)*
**Sherwood Park Primary School**


## I KEEP LOSING MY GLASSES

I keep losing my glasses,
I don't know where I put them,
I don't know if I put them over here or over there,
It is so hard to find them!
I have looked in my garden and at school,
But then I saw my glasses case and I opened it,
I saw my glasses and put them somewhere safe!

*Cassandra Underwood (9)*
**Sherwood Park Primary School**

## WILDLIFE

W eeny, weeny, little animals
I nsects they are called
L adybirds, ants and
D ragonflies too
L izards hissing with their tongues
I n the wildlife they have been
F oxes scrounging in your bin
E nd of the day is when they will be seen.

*Amy Gates  (10)*
**Sherwood Park Primary School**


## WHAT IS THIS COLOUR?

What is gold?
Stars are gold with the new and old
What is red? A light is red
The light that makes you go to bed
What is blue? The sea is blue
With the wind too
What is green? A plant is green
From the tiny bean.

*Sheniz Batmaz  (8)*
**Sherwood Park Primary School**

## RAIN

Rain dribbles down the school windows
*Pitter-patter, pitter-patter* on the roof
Rain is pouring
It's turning into hailstones
*Bang, bang, bang!*
It's like the sky is roaring
The sound is dreadful
The hailstones are rattling on the roof
*Pitter-patter, pitter-patter* all day long.

**Christopher Spencer  (10)**
**Sherwood Park Primary School**


## RAIN

When the rain is out to play, it falls and
Sprinkles from the sky with its beautiful
Dripping sound on the floor when it falls
I like it when I look out of the window
Even though I can't go out to play, *pitter-patter*
*Pitter-patter* all day long.

**Samuel Bell  (10)**
**Sherwood Park Primary School**

## WATERFALLS

Waterfalls trickle and shimmer in the sun
As it splashes, the colours of the rainbow show
The water at the bottom of the waterfall
When it's passed the rocks it flows
At the end of the waterfall
It bubbles and froths around the rocks
By the waterfall it is always peaceful
As the white bubbly water falls
The rocks gleam as the water bounces off after hitting them.

*Katie Lawton (10)*
*Sherwood Park Primary School*


## THE DANCE

She danced all day
She danced all night
But on the way
With such delight

She met a prince
In the night
He asked her to dance
And be his bride.

*Rebecca Howard (9)*
*Sherwood Park Primary School*

## FAIRIES

Just be careful
Do not stand in a Gallitrap
It's dangerous as can be
Your spirit can be taken away
From the fairies that are free
As fairies sprinkle magic dust
Over the lands and sea
As every sprinkle settles on the ground
More Gallitraps there will be.

*Natasha Cockerill (10)*
*Sherwood Park Primary School*


## HOLIDAYS ARE FUN

Holidays give you time to play
And time to be with your family
The times when you play
And have ice cream
The children play on the grass
Some run fast, some run slow
When you win prizes you have a surprise
The growing of flowers.

*Charlotte Ryan (9)*
*Sherwood Park Primary School*

## SNOW, SNOW, SNOW

Snow is falling,
Icing sugar sprinkled everywhere,
Starry glitter drifting down
Calling children to come and play.
Sledging down hills,
Hat, scarf, nose, build a snowman.
Snowballs flying across the sky,
Slipping, sliding on the slippery ice.
The sun is rising
I wish I didn't have to say this
But 'Bye-bye snow.'

*Lucy Ainsworth  (9)*
*Sherwood Park Primary School*


## MY FOOTBALL CRAZY

I am mad
I used to play football when I was a lad
But sometimes I've very, very sad
My mum tells me I am tough
But I said, 'I'm skinny and weak'
And sometimes I'm really a pest
My old granny says I'm really scruffy
Sometimes I get stressed
I sometimes get an ice cream
Oh! Stuff the ice cream
I'm playing football.

*Ronnie Cruddas  (9)*
*Sherwood Park Primary School*

## MY PRETTY DAFFODILS

My pretty daffodils are the best in the world,
They love the sun and they love getting watered,
They follow the sun wherever it goes,
They follow the sun wherever it goes.

My daffodils are really bright,
They shine at night because of their colours
With their lovely pretty heads,
My daffodils smell the best,
My daffodils are the best.

I love my daffodils,
I love my daffodils.

*Jessica Hollands  (8)*
**Sherwood Park Primary School**


## A SILENT POEM

I can hear bees
Buzzing in the trees
I can hear fish
Eating out of a dish
I can hear the monkey
Sitting on a donkey
I can hear a dog
Running on a log
I can hear a snake
Eating a cake
I can hear people
Writing a line
I like the rabbits
That have lots of habits.

*Lauren Gorey  (8)*
**Sherwood Park Primary School**

## WHAT IS WHITE?

What is white? A goose is white
With fluffy feathers.
What is blue? The sky is blue
On a summer's day.
What is green? The grass is green.
What is red? A tomato is red,
Juicy and yummy.
What is yellow? A sunflower is yellow,
Shiny and bright.
What is brown? A dog is brown,
Cute and furry.

*Abbie Smith (7)*
**Sherwood Park Primary School**


## MILLWALL ARE THE BEST

Millwall are the best
Better than the rest
If we had a fight
It'd be in the night

Dennis Wise is very small
He didn't like people who were tall
When he got a yellow card
Then he was barred.

*Ben Foley (10)*
**Sherwood Park Primary School**

## TILO THE T-REX

There was a big T-Rex
Who ate a dinosaur
And when he ate it
He finished it off with a *roar!*

He snuck through the grass and the rusty leaves
To find another one
All the dinosaurs ran away
Because they heard he fell on his bum!

His name is Tilo
Big and fat
He's bigger than a little boy
He's bigger than a rat!

He walks along the dusty sand
To find a dinosaur
He snuck up on a juicy one
And killed it with a roar!

*Siobhan Tarran (9)*
*Sherwood Park Primary School*


## MONKEY, MONKEY

Monkey, monkey jumping on the wall
Monkey, monkey jumping on the school
Monkey, monkey jumping on a tree
Monkey, monkey jumping on my knee
Monkey, monkey I love you.

*Rianna Hughes (7)*
*Sherwood Park Primary School*

## CYCLONES

Cyclones coming down your street,
Swiping everyone off their feet,
Smashing the buildings down and down,
Ruining your 'homeful' town.

Made by heavy rain and wind,
Twirling round like an opening tin,
It comes around twisting people's mouths,
Ripping off animals' tails!

They are very cold and wet as well,
Nobody can even tell,
Because cyclones, twisters, hurricanes too,
Are all the same, the names are cool!

If your town is the place for them,
Then watch out kids and ladies and men,
It could be coming right this way,
Just hope and pray this is your lucky day!

*Jessica Pezzolesi (10)*
*Sherwood Park Primary School*


## ME AND MY BLACK EYE

I have a black eye
As dark as a tunnel
I feel like everyone
Is staring at me!
First it went purple
Then black
Now it feels like I've got
A needle in my chest.

*Marcus Albertsen (8)*
*Sherwood Park Primary School*

## FLOWERS, FLOWERS

Flowers, flowers
In the air
Flowers, flowers
Everywhere
Flowers, flowers
In a pair
Flowers, flowers
In a den
Flowers, flowers
On the chair
Flowers, flowers
In the garden
Flowers, flowers
In the road
Flowers, flowers
Follow me everywhere.

*Ellie Roberts  (9)*
**Sherwood Park Primary School**


## FOOTBALL FEVER

I love football, it's the best thing in the world,
Arsenal, Chelsea, Charlton, West Ham are all good teams,
Football season's already started so they're all gonna work hard.
Sweat, injuries, glory, failure, all parts of football,
The best bits are the trophies and cups.
You win together and lose together,
So it's excellent when you win,
But it's also not too bad when you lose,
It teaches you a lesson and then, you will sing
And that is what makes football so great,
I love football, it's the best thing in the world!

*Alex Jones  (8)*
**Sherwood Park Primary School**

## I HAVE A BIG FAMILY

I have a nice mummy
And my room is scrummy
I have a big dad
And he makes me mad
I have a brother called Joe
He's as ugly as Po
Then there is Sam
He's as annoying as sloppy ham
And there's Billy
He's really silly
And me
But there's nothing that rhymes with me!
And also Mealie
Who likes doing wheelies!
But then there's a baby on the way
Which keeps me at bay
And that's my family.

*George Rixon  (8)*
**Sherwood Park Primary School**


## FOOTBALL CRAZY

I've been football crazy
Since I was 2 years old
I've played all types of football
Beach football
Underwater football
Ordinary football
Club football,
*Football!*

*Daniel Warman  (8)*
**Sherwood Park Primary School**

## MY SISTER

At home I've got a sister
Sometimes she's a pest
She's got a teacher called Mr Chester
But really she's the best
I love my sister as much as she loves me
She's the best as all can be
Her favourite food is spaghetti Bolognese
Her favourite drink is cherry lemonade
She likes school, she really is cool
I love my sister and she loves me too
And believe me, she's not a fool.

*Charanpreet Plahi (8)*
*Sherwood Park Primary School*


## MY SISTER AND ME

My sister and me,
My little, tiny sister,
She always bullies me,
Always takes my felt pens,
Losing all my good things,
Pinching all my T-shirts,
That my mum bought me,
Sometimes I wish I was outdoors,
Where she couldn't find me!
*Can you help me, please?*

*Chlóe Witton (9)*
*Sherwood Park Primary School*

## FOOTBALL CRAZY

The beautiful game,
Defending horror,
Fearsome free-kicks and goal crazy,
Corners,
Lights,
Teams,
Sponsors,
Sideboards
And fans,
Nets,
Stadium,
Commentator,
Pitch,
Players,
Referee in black,
Linesmen,
Goal kicks,
Managers,
Flags,
Dug-out,
Eighteen yard line,
Six yard line,
Goal line,
Posts,
Bars,
Suffering substitutes,
Midfield madness,
*Football!*

***George Usher  (9)***
**Sherwood Park Primary School**

## My Cousin, William

My cousin, William, is a pest
Shall I tell you all the rest?
He likes a lolly
When he is playing with tomboy, Polly
He calls me Dott
But I am called Scott
He is two and a half
He likes to walk down the path
His mum is called Sue
But we call her Aunty Doo
He has a sister called Gemma
Who plays with Heather!

*Scott Shergold  (8)*
**Sherwood Park Primary School**


## Boys!

I like boys,
Short boys,
Tall boys,
Boys with brown hair,
Boys with blond hair,
I like cute boys,
Funny boys,
I love some boys,
Yes, some boys love you,
Some don't,
But I know,
I really like boys!

*Chloe Beckett  (8)*
**Sherwood Park Primary School**

## HAVING FUN WITH ANIMALS

Animals, animals
They are great
Having fun playing with animals
Cats, rats and also bats
They are fun, everyone

Kittens playing with mittens, they are so cute
I love playing with my hamster, Hunny
I love playing with my cat called Lucky

Animals playing in the bright sun
Animals playing in the sight of the sun
Animals, animals.

*Rebecca Freathy (8)*
**Sherwood Park Primary School**


## I LOVE GINGER

I love Ginger, he's the best
Miaow, miaow, he follows me around the house
His tail wags
He lays on my tummy
What shall I do?
Curl up and fall asleep
Miaow, miaow
Cat's cute
Miaow, miaow
I love you Ginger
I love you Ginger
Ginger is beautiful
Ginger, Ginger
Ginger is sweet!

*Hannah Bishop (9)*
**Sherwood Park Primary School**

## FIREWORK NIGHT

*Bang, crackle, pop*
The night fills with pixie dust
Rockets fly up high
Some are quite lovely
Some are quite bright
In the ink-black sky

*Bang, crackle, pop*
Smoky air everywhere
The bonfire burning
Flames high and roaring
Children excited running about
All they can do is scream and shout

*Bang, crackle, pop*
Falling lights like twinkling stars
Popping, popping all around
The last sparks of fire fall to the ground
It's the end of the night
There's no more sound.

**Sacha Surgenor  (9)**
*The Schools At Somerhill*


## WHAT IS THE WIND

Loud howls of a wolf,
Piercing the chill night air.

Air from the giant's nostrils,
Making the trees quiver in its might.

It is the sign of wrath,
Shot from the Devil flying by.

**Poppy Morris  (9)**
*The Schools At Somerhill*

## AUTUMN

In autumn I hear the leaves crisping and crackling
The wind waving like mad twirling everywhere
The acorns floating down from the trees with a loud thump

I see bronze conkers hanging from the trees
They swing from side to side
I see smoke spinning out of the chimneys

I feel the wind cutting through my face like glass
I feel the coldness right next to me
I feel stuffy with my hat and coat on me like a hairy dog.

*Phoebe Loveland  (9)*
*The Schools At Somerhill*


## COME BACK

I see my mother, she's coming
In the mist
She's running like the wind
She's saying my name, Maisie, Maisie
She's getting closer now
I hear her

Now she's here, I don't know how
It's like a special day
A magical day
I am not alone anymore.

*Maisie Taylor  (10)*
*The Schools At Somerhill*

## FIREWORKS

Swishing, swirling all around
Hopping, jumping, upside down
Catherine wheels are everywhere
Jumping jacks in the air

Sparkles and jewels
Light up the night
It's a race to get to
The top of the sky

Big booms and crackles
And noises I never knew
Happiness, joy, love
I guess that means you.

***Catherine Mogan  (10)***
*The Schools At Somerhill*


## SANTA

Down the chimney he comes
I hear him laughing
I hear him hum
As he eats his mince pies and drinks his wine
It is almost morning, oh I can't wait
He fills the stockings up one by one
I hear him go up, up and away
It is silent as the day comes.

***Alexandra Montgomery  (10)***
*The Schools At Somerhill*

## DEEP IN THE WOODS

Deep in the woods,
Deep in the woods,
The skylark sings
Above the evergreen trees.

Deep in the woods,
Deep in the woods,
The hedgehog scuttles
Amongst the gathering leaves.

Deep in the woods,
Deep in the woods,
The fox slinks
On the moist ground.

Deep in the woods,
Deep in the woods,
The deer gallop
Between the slender trees.

Deep in the woods,
Deep in the woods,
There are many secrets
I cannot tell or know.

*Emily Barrett  (11)*
**The Schools At Somerhill**

## MY PUPPY

Small and white
She whimpers at night
Her little black nose
Feels wet on my toes

Her bark is not loud
Nor ferocious or proud
She is playful and fun
With each and everyone

Her toys are soft slippers
Her teeth, little nippers
Oh my puppy I am dotty
For she is little Lottie.

***Chloe Mitchell (9)***
*The Schools At Somerhill*


## SHEEP

Sheep are stupid and crazy,
They munch on grass all day,
Sometimes appear lazy,
Other times frisky and gay.

Their fleece is white and woolly,
I think they look quite snug
And when it's very cold outside,
I'd quite like one to hug.

Their faces are peculiar,
They have a big fat tummy,
But when we eat our Sunday lunch,
I find they are quite scrummy.

***Lara Staffurth (10)***
*The Schools At Somerhill*

## THE SNAKE
*(Inspired by Brian Moses)*

He slithers through
A clump of grass,
Making a swishing sound,
The sun blazes down,
On his dusty scales,
As he slides over arid ground.

He casts an eye,
A malevolent stare
And grimaces in the baking day.
His tail whips,
Along the cracked earth,
Where many eggs lay.

At the flash of lighting,
He grabs his prey,
In the wink of an eye
And travels away
From the vast pile
Like a secret spy.

*Juliet Cornick (11)*
*The Schools At Somerhill*


## MY SUPER GERBIL

My super gerbil is as fierce as a teacher giving out detentions
And as fat as an elephant which swallowed a hippo
It is as fast as a snake on my brother's skateboard
And as hungry as a mum on a diet
It is as friendly as a butterfly eating some leaves
And as noisy as a firework display going off twice
I was really fond of my super gerbil until it ate my *mum!*

*Kathryn Cross (10)*
*The Schools At Somerhill*

252

# FIREWORKS

The 5th of November I'll always remember
It was a dark and cold night
The crowd waited in suspense
There was a loud *bang*

I jumped back in fright
Crimson, yellow then white
As fireworks lit up the night sky
Rockets followed each other one by one
Flashing, whizzing and spiralling at a great height
The bangers glittering, shooting up, up and away

There goes the catherine wheel
Spitting sparks through the air
The sky is bright with many colours
Smoke obscured the velvet sky
The colourful lights flickered and went out
We were left in darkness once again.

***Katherine Molloy (11)***
*The Schools At Somerhill*


# WE LOVE EACH OTHER

I love my mum and she loves me,
We like to go and climb some trees.
We go to the park, when it gets dark
And go to the shops to get ice creams.

I love my sister and she loves me,
She takes me to town, to have some tea,
We like to go shopping, to get some clothes,
When people get into fights, she sticks up her nose.

***Becky Scott (10)***
*The Schools At Somerhill*

## THE FUNKY MONKEY

The monkey owns a disco,
In faraway Bombay
And he sits there playing his bongos,
While chattering away.

He called his friend the zebra,
On his Nokia 5204,
'Would you bring your beautiful stripes' he said,
'To add to the great décor?'

Next he emailed the crocodile
At gruesomegrin.com,
'Come smile at my disco, reflect the light,
But you must promise not to bite.'

Then he faxed the elephant,
On his funky fax machine,
'We need your trunk as a microphone
Or the karaoke singers will all go home.'

He broadcast to the jungle,
On satellite TV,
'Animals come to my disco,
For a crazy, wild party!'

The zebra was a great success,
Showing off her stripy dress,
The elephant was really proud,
Because his sound system was extremely loud.
The only one to spoil the do,
Was the crocodile who began to chew . . .
'Help, help, the décor's being eaten!'
*Snap! Snap! Snap!*

***Alexandra Hitch  (11)***
**The Schools At Somerhill**

## MY MONSTER MOUSE

My monster mouse is as heavy as a giant baby
And as long as a great blue whale
He is as fast as a cheetah racing at the speed of light
And as strong as a hurricane's gale
He is as noisy as a howling monkey screaming into a microphone
And his teeth are the biggest razors
He is as fierce as a moody shark
And his eyes are like lasers

I really admire my monster mouse
I adore his babies too
But they don't like me!

*Argh!*

**Caroline Goring  (9)**
*The Schools At Somerhill*


## I LOST A FRIEND TODAY

I lost a special friend today,
She meant a lot to me.
I tried to pull her back,
But she had to leave me behind.
I have so many memories of us together,
In a tree eating ice cream,
Doing work together,
Even walking together,
I knew this day would come,
She left me, it felt blurred in the sand,
I lost a friend today
And she meant a lot to me!

***Victoria Young  (10)***
*The Schools At Somerhill*

## MY AUNT

My aunt is as big as a monster and she looks like one too!
She walks around in a big T-shirt all day
And at bedtime she hides and runs away
To meet her friends who scare me away!

She never comes to visit
She never comes to play
I want to see my weird old aunt
And meet her friends today

I want to see her friend
Who has a giant tongue
That could stretch from her to Africa
That would be really fun

But this is just a fantasy
This is just a dream
She is really *boring*
She sits around watching TV.

*Ella Darbyshire (9)*
**The Schools At Somerhill**


## THE MOON

Moonlight, moonlight shining so bright,
He looks like a crescent,
He has his friends who are the stars,
Who help him to light up the sky.
He sometimes likes to hide behind the clouds,
So you cannot see his reflection.
In the daytime he likes to sleep
And you never hear a little peep.

*Natalie Thompson (10)*
**The Schools At Somerhill**

## UNTITLED

What? Who? When?
Where?

What?
Why are these people looking at me?

Who?
Who is he to tell me what to do?

When?
When did you hear a boy say he liked me?

Where?
Where am I now and where will I be?

***Charlotte Daniels  (9)***
**The Schools At Somerhill**


## AUTUMN DAYS

Autumn days never stop,
They go on and on and on.
The wind blows, the trees rustle,
Golden leaves, rosy apples.

The leaves float, glide, spin and swirl,
Into a heap of scarlet shapes.
The birds begin their hibernation,
And there's silence in the woods.

The wind cuts through my face when I'm outside,
Like a razor slashing through me,
It blows and splinters,
Then I stand there in the middle of the park, cold!

***Rose Maclachlan  (8)***
**The Schools At Somerhill**

# THE EXCITING DAYS OF CHRISTMAS

Sweets, treats, tinsel and presents,
It's Christmas Eve!
No more school and fun on the way,
Presents are wrapped and under the tree,
The fairy lights are as bright as can be,
Late night games and chocolate galore,
I just can't wait anymore.

Sweets, treats, tinsel and presents,
It's Christmas morning!
Kisses and hugs and run down the stairs,
Yes, he's been - crumbs left and *presents!*
Tear the wrapping paper off and shriek with delight,
Rush to tidy the family are due,
We're so excited and the dogs are too!

Sweets, treats, tinsel and presents,
It's dinnertime, what a good smell,
Plate after plate of delicious feasts,
*Bang* goes the crackers and jokes are told,
Hey, Uncle John, don't forget your hat,
I can't wait for the pudding and cake,
*Mmm*, delicious. Mum said it took hours to bake.

*Heather Barnett (9)*
*The Schools At Somerhill*

## SPIRIT

Slowly, she yawns and stretches her arms,
Her glistening lips moving,
Her wispy hair swings to and fro,
Curls covering her pale face,
An ivy crown entangled on her head,
An emerald silk draped on her neck,
A thick velvet colour of cream,
Wrapped tightly round her fragile body,
Thin stripes of reed bounding her feet,
As they creep across the plain,
Her eyes, a deep turquoise,
Bore into the sky,
Almost as if she wished,
It would swallow her,
Her dainty fingers rubbed against,
The tree's rough bark,
Leaving a thin, crimson scratch,
Upon the white-as-snow hand,
Suddenly she freezes, as if ice bound her,
Her arms and legs turning chestnut colour,
Her head spun rapidly, then it stopped,
But as a leafy object,
Not a woman standing there,
But a sapling just growing.

*Courtney Jiskoot (10)*
**The Schools At Somerhill**

259

# THE TRIP TO THE MALL

Humpty Dumpty sat on the stool,
When Little Miss Muffet gave him a call,
He picked up the phone,
With one big groan,
Said Little Miss Muffet,
Who was sitting on a tuffet,
'We will all remember
That day in November
When Jack Horner
Deserted his corner,
Then set off to the mall
To set up his stall.'
Said Humpty Dumpty
Who had stopped being grumpy,
'I will give you a lolly
From my parrot, Polly.'
Humpty Dumpty leapt off his stool
And sprinted to the mall,
Where he met Bo Peep
Buying food for her sheep,
Humpty had had a very long day,
So he went to sleep and didn't wake up until May.

*Alice Goodwin  (11)*
**The Schools At Somerhill**

## IF I WERE A SHAPE

If I were a shape
I'd be a cube,
I'd be a dice rolling on a board of Monopoly,
Intending to show a six.
I'd be a block of ice chilling in a freezer
Or bobbing in a drink.
I'd be a chunk of cheese pronged onto a
Kebab stick, ready to eat,
If I were a cube.

If I were a shape
I'd be a sphere,
I'd be a juicy orange, succulent and ripe,
Sitting in a fruit bowl.
I'd be a football signed by Posh and Becks.
I'd be a raindrop falling from the sky,
All wet and cold,
If I were a sphere.

If I were a shape
I'd be a cylinder,
I'd be a poster rolled up
And tied with a blue rubber band.
I'd be a tin of pineapple,
Being emptied into a Christmas trifle.
I'd be a drum being hit at an African tribe festival,
If I were a cylinder.

But maybe . . .
I don't want to change at all!

*Emily Wilkes  (9)*
**The Schools At Somerhill**

# IF I WERE . . .

I'd be a sphere,
I'd be a football with David Beckham scoring,
I'd be a lollipop fizzing in my mouth,
If I were a sphere.

If I were a circle,
I'd be a tyre of a golf GTI,
Whizzing around and around the road,
I'd be a CD spinning in a new CD player,
I'd be a clock that was ticking away the time,
If I were a circle.

If I were a rectangle,
I'd be a bar of chocolate from my aunt,
Just waiting to be eaten,
I'd be an ace of hearts sitting in the pack of cards,
I'd be a football pitch,
With Chelsea scoring never-ending goals,
If I were a rectangle.

If I were a star
I'd be Britney Spears.

*Amy Devitt  (9)*
*The Schools At Somerhill*


# DREAMING

I always dream of a faraway land,
Where everybody lends a hand.
I love to be slothful and pick some flowers
And do artistic drawings, for hours.
I love to visit my lovely farm,
Where none of the animals cause you harm.

*Saskia Lightwood  (10)*
*The Schools At Somerhill*

## PORTRAIT OF A DRAGON

If I were an artist,
I'd paint a portrait of a dragon.

For his head
I'd use a grinning crocodile's head,
Smiling at me like a monkey.

His eyes would be sparkling rubies,
Glistening in the moonlight.

For his eyebrows I would use pieces of jet-black coal,
Winking all the time.

For his body I'd use a tree,
Rough and splodgy like painted, crumpled paper.

His toes and claws would be like bananas
On endless purple vines.

For the colour of his body
I'd use grass, rubies, tulips, marble
And all the colours of the rainbow.

*Eleanor Shotton  (9)*
*The Schools At Somerhill*


## MY DAZZLING DRAGON

My dazzling dragon is as big as a Concorde
And as wide as the fattest man,
It is as hungry as a family of lions
And as noisy as a giant running,
It is so strong that it can hold 10 elephants
And as quick as a man falling from the sky,
The only problem is, he was so quick,
He ran off and I couldn't catch him!

*Francesca Maffei  (10)*
*The Schools At Somerhill*

## How To Make Spring

It needs . . .

A warm sunshine like a beaming smile,
A deep shaded carpet of bluebells like a calm sea,
Little buds like beads on a string,
Birds singing their songs like the distant whistle of the wind
in a valley,
Daffodils with their trumpets up like they're in a royal palace,
Baby lambs skipping like a soft bucking bronco,
Baby chicks moving their heads as they walk like they're
dancing to music,
That's what you need to make spring!

*Katie Hoskin  (8)*
**The Schools At Somerhill**


## How To Make Spring

You need . . .
A carpet of bluebells like calm purple seas,
A ray of warm sunshine like a daffodil glowing in the blue sky,
Birds twittering like a harp playing softly,
An early evening sunshine as relaxing as being in a spa,
Buds of snowdrops like snowflakes slowly drifting to the ground,
Blossoms growing like deep red cherries sitting on a china plate,
Light refreshing showers sparkling like the sea,
Grass as green as a succulent apple.

*Jessica Hawkes  (8)*
**The Schools At Somerhill**

## MY BEST FRIEND

He's looking old and dishevelled,
Worn out by so much love,
His beak is bald, his eyes are blind,
Legs limp and tail gone,
The squeaker in his wing
No longer talks to me.

His body has lost its plumpness,
Worn out by so much love,
In times of crisis he's always there,
To reassure and calm,
He never asks for anything
Or favours in return.

Mum's magic thread
Has saved the day
And washed away my tears
And kept my duck,
My bestest friend
With me for years and years.

*Georgia Lewis-Smith  (10)*
**The Schools At Somerhill**


## MY DESK

My desk is very messy and sometimes very clean,
When my desk is messy it eats all the work that I have done
And I get told off when it does that,
When my desk is messy it shouts out all the rude words to my teacher,
When my desk is messy it steals all my pens,
When my desk is tidy it just sits there,
This is a warning, keep your desk tidy!

*Sophie Edwards  (9)*
**The Schools At Somerhill**

# WHAT IS SPRING?

A new life of inspiration
An end to the days of blankness
A freeness feeling in the air
The beginning after the end
A new start of generations
What could this beauty be?
Why, it could only be spring.

A gentle feeling, welcoming
A new feeling to the world
A chance to start again
After the time of darkness
A new feeling in the heart
What could this love be?
Why, it could only be spring.

A new vision to the eye
A new sound to the ear
A new inspiration to the mind
After the time of black and white
A world of colour opens
What could this colour be?
Why, it could only be spring.

*Emma de Mattos  (10)*
**The Schools At Somerhill**

## My Dog, Seve!

My dog, Seve,
He is rather heavy!
He is black with floppy ears,
He is not very quiet,
He causes a riot
And always chases deer!

He is a black lab
And as a pet he is fab,
I take him to the park,
But we are both scared of the dark!

I love my dog, Seve,
Even though he is heavy!

*Grace Whatman  (9)*
*The Schools At Somerhill*